From The Polar Night
To Eternal Light

This narrative of love, courage and deep faith spans more than half a century and some 10,000 miles. From wartime Norway to the quiet beauty of Southern Oregon, Inger Schneider tells of common tribulations in today's world and of the triumphs that are so rare.

Inger's comfortable and unassuming relationship with her God, her devotion to her family as well as her absolute faith in the outcome of tomorrow, propel her out of the ordinary and into the realm of the unique.

Within these pages is a story of a life worth knowing and a message worth hearing.

Toni R. Bergene
Ashland, Oregon
December 1988

From The Polar Night
To Eternal Light

from my ❤ *to your* ❤

By

Inger Marie Schneider

Foreword by Hans J. Schneider
Cover designed by Brian Freeman

Published by
World Wide Publishing Corporation
P.O. Box 105
Ashland, Oregon 97520-0105

From the Polar Night to Eternal Light
By Inger Marie Schneider
Copyright © 1989 by Inger Marie Schneider. All rights reserved. No part of this book may be reproduced or transmitted in any form or by any means, electronic or mechanical, including photocopying, recording or by any information storage and retrieval system, without permission in writing from the publisher.

Published by World Wide Publishing Corporation, P.O. Box 105, Ashland, Oregon 97520.

Printed in the United States of America

ISBN 0-930294-16-5 (Softbound)

Library of Congress Cataloging-in-Publication Data

Schneider, Inger Marie, 1932–
   From the polar night to eternal light/by Inger Marie Schneider.
      p.   cm.
   Summary: The author describes the role of God in her life from her childhood in Norway through adult years in the United States.
   ISBN 0-930294-16-5 (soft)
   1. Schneider, Inger Marie, 1932–   . 2. Christian biography—
—United States.   [1. Schneider, Inger Marie, 1932–
2. Christian biography.]   I. Title.
BR1725.S373A3   1989
209'.2'4--dc19
[B]
[92]   88-38885
                                                 CIP
                                                 AC

A warm and hearty thanks to my husband and children for their help and encouragement. A special thanks to Mr. Wayne Paulsen for correcting the English, and to Mrs. Lois Wright for typing the manuscript.

How glad and thankful I am to Wanna Walker for typesetting and giving me the final help to get the book printed, and to Brian Freeman for the cover design and map work.

I appreciate each of you for your love and encouragement.

Your friend,

Inger M. Schneider

Inger M. Schneider

A WORD ABOUT THE AUTHOR

Inger Marie Schneider was born November 5, 1932 in Gamvik, Norway, the northernmost village of Europe. She grew up in the "Land of the Midnight Sun." Her life is an unbelievable story of survival in the face of suffering and persecution.

She left Norway in 1956 to start a new life in America. In 1957 she married Sigvart Wathne. Roy, Tom and Helen Marie were the children of this marriage. Her husband was killed in an industrial accident in April 1964.

Inger Marie married Hans J. Schneider, Christian evangelist and publisher, in October 1967. Josef John and Rose Sharon are the children of this marriage.

She has worked for World Wide Evangelism since 1967, speaking at meetings and sending out Bibles and Bible tracts to many, many lands. Since 1980 Inger has worked for World Wide Publishing Corporation.

Inger Marie Schneider is listed in the 16th Edition of Who's Who of American Women.

Her avocations are skiing, traveling and camping.

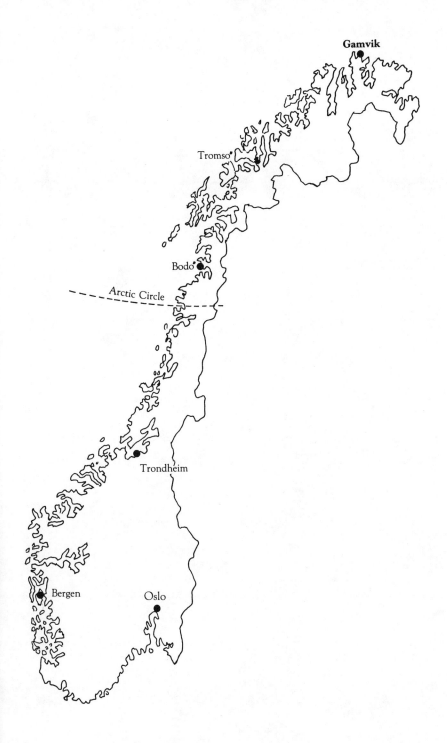

This book is dedicated to the
Glory of God

Contents

Preface

Drip, drip, drip, cold water was coming down my back. It was pitch dark and I could not remember where I was. Then it dawned on me that I was in a little "puppy tent" on the Oregon coast with my four younger children. The evening had just been beautiful. We had hiked on the beach, built a nice campfire and gone to bed. Why this change of weather? The wind was blowing and it was raining hard. The tent had sagged in the middle and of course it had to leak. I checked on the children and they were dry and sleeping soundly. If I only had not forgotten the flashlight, we could break up camp and go home, but without any light it was impossible to pack. So I decided to stay put, and make the best of it. I quietly prayed and talked to the Lord.

Then He asked me, "Inger, when will you write your book?"

"Oh no, Lord! You really got me pinned down, why should You also ask me to write? You know I cannot write, and You know how I spell, I make a mess out of the English language." But the pressure was on, I knew that none of the excuses I made was good. I had used the same reasons for not writing, when ladies would ask me, after I had given my testimony in their groups; also, other people had requested the same, when I told them about my early years beyond the Arctic Circle. Not to forget my sweet husband and children, for they would ask me, too. But I always put it off. "Look around," I would say, "see how many books we have in this world, they don't need another book." So I had been able to get away with it.

But now the Lord was speaking, and it was different. He was not speaking in a loud voice. When you know Him, you know His voice and His dealing with you. Finally I said, "Yes, Lord, one day I will write." And in the back of my mind I saw myself as a white-haired old grandma writing, the house quiet, and all my chores done.

A peace came over me as I said "yes." The daylight came creeping in through the branches. A new day had started.

This happened about two years ago. Now again my husband and I went on a speaking tour to Portland, Oregon. We were guests on a River of Life television program called "Branches." Doug Hildebrand and his wife Joan interviewed us. After the program Doug said firmly, "You should write your story, Inger."

So here I am, by the help of God, trying to bring glory to His name.

1

Born and Raised in "The Land of the Midnight Sun"

My Dad

L et us start at the very beginning. Fasten your seatbelt and come with me on a trip to a land beyond the arctic circle, to the tip-top of Norway. This part of the country is known as "The Land of the Midnight Sun"—but the "midnight sun" is mostly for tourists. They do not know about the Polar Night, when it is dark almost around the clock. In December you have only a couple of hours of daylight. The winter is long. I often say, "We have nine months of winter, and three months of bad skiing."

Gamvik, my hometown is the northernmost village in Europe. It is located out on a point, and beyond is the ocean as far as you can see. Fishing is good and most people earn their livelihoods from fishing.

I was born the seventh in a family of eight children. It was a stormy November night when I saw light for the first time. Perhaps the storm was there to testify that my life was not going to be a bed of roses.

Father was a fisherman and worked almost day and night trying to support such a large family. He was not a Christian, but I know in my heart he respected my mother's God. I learned a great deal from Dad; he was a brave fisherman.

Besides fishing, Dad took care of three lighthouses. One of my earliest memories is going with him to tend the lights. Often the snow was knee deep, as I trotted behind him, trying to walk in his footsteps. Dad took very good care of his lighthouses. I can still see him polishing the windows inside and outside, filling the kerosene lamp, trimming the wick and washing the chimney. Then he lighted the lamp and watched it carefully until it was established, not too low and not too high. If the flame was too low, it would not give enough light. Too high, it had a tendency to smoke up the chimney. I often got impatient and said, "Daddy, why don't you hurry?" But no, he did not hurry, for he knew the importance of those lights. I often saw him at night blowing on our frozen window until a little spot thawed so he could look out and see how his lighthouses were coming along.

In the evening we ran to the dock waiting for Dad to come home. Often the ocean churned wildly and big waves slammed their power against the seashore and made it tremble. We could spot Dad's boat like a nutshell far out. We watched and prayed as Dad sailed his boat closer and closer until he reached the shore with his beard and clothing full of icicles. His eyes had the same color as the ocean, but I could notice a touch of steel in them. One more time he wrestled with the ocean and won. Many of his friends and his own brother drowned. I can still remember Grandma sitting in our kitchen looking out the window, whispering, "The ocean giveth and taketh." How true it was!

My Mom

Mother was a wonderful believer. She had heard the good news as we read in Isaiah 9:2, 6: *"The people that walked in darkness have seen a great light: they that dwell in the land of the shadow of death, upon them hath the light shined. For unto us a child is born, unto us a son is given: and the government shall be upon his shoulder: and his name shall be called Wonderful, Counselor, The mighty God, The everlasting Father, The Prince of Peace."* In her childlike faith she blessed the food on our table and also the hay in the barn; and somehow there was enough to go around. Mom was always talking to the

Lord as she worked happily in the home. Even as small children we could see the Lord's blessing upon our lives.

2
War Years

One day when I came home from school, mother was crying. "Why do you cry?" I asked.

"We are having war, and your oldest brother must go to fight."

Although I could not fully understand what war meant, I just felt it must be very serious. Soon the German soldiers came to our village. Life was rough so far north; now it was even rougher.

Our Playgrounds Turn Into Forts, Our Fishing Areas Into Mined Battlefields

Our schoolhouse was taken from us. From now on we had to go from house to house for schooling. They made a fort out of our playground. From my bedroom window I could see cannons and machine guns almost hanging into our backyard. When they were shooting, the whole house shook and many times the windows were broken.

Sometimes big convoys would pass by. We could count about twelve to fourteen boats in one convoy. Since we lived on a point, it was a perfect place for submarines to lie in wait. Often we saw boats blow up and sink. Sometimes the oil or gas would burn for days. The rescue boats later rushed out and picked up dead soldiers. I can so well remember the impact as I watched the trucks going by my home loaded with dead soldiers. The seagulls had eaten out their eyes.

At night sometimes we were awakened by air raids and had to run to the cellar, never knowing if we would live another day.

The Lord Provides

Yes, life was dangerous—but how wonderfully the Lord supplied all our needs! For five years we had to stand in long lines to get food, and often we could not get any. Clothes and shoes were next to impossible to buy. Poor mother! . . . she was mending all the time. One set of "longjohns" had 38 patches; soon you could not tell the difference between the original and the patches. I had a green crocheted dress. Every fall when school started, mother asked me to put on the green dress. She measured how much I had grown and then she crocheted on some more. "This will take you through another year," she said happily. I cannot remember how many years that dress lasted, but I know it was a long, long time. And to this day I cannot stand a certain green color.

Shoes were not that easy to fix. One day, when I was in great need of some shoes, we heard the news that Sweden had donated some for the most needy children. The teacher was going to give them to us during lunch break. I was so excited I could not concentrate on anything he said; all I thought of were shoes. Finally the hour arrived. The teacher brought in some burlap sacks, ripped them open with his pocketknife, and dumped them on the floor. And there, to our big surprise, was a heap of huge military shoes! My, were they ever big. At first we all thought that it was a joke—but it wasn't. We had to wear those big shoes. That day when the children walked home from school, it looked as though a whole army had marched by, as we turned around and saw the big footprints in the snow. The shoes were not fancy, but they kept us warm and humble.

At Gun Point

During those five years of war we had to cover up the windows whenever we burned a light. If a small ray of light escaped, a soldier knocked on the door and said, "Verdunkeln, verdunkeln," which meant, "Make it dark." One night a few soldiers came into our house. With a gun pointed at Dad, they said, "You are spies, you signaled by light to our enemies." In

German some of the older children asked when it was that they saw the light. "About 8 o'clock in the evening," they answered. Then Mom and Dad remembered that it was the time when they had done the chores and carried a small lantern to the barn. The soldiers left our house without hurting us, but warned, "Be careful, don't do it again."

Deadly Toys

Sad was the day when two little neighbor girls played at the seashore. They thought they had found a really interesting toy. It proved to be a hand grenade and when they pulled the string, the grenade exploded in their laps. One girl was killed instantly, while the other lived for two or three hours.

One boy hiking along the seashore saw an object that he had never seen before. He took a rock and knocked on it to check if it would make a sound. It was a big horn mine and he hit the horn. The mine went off and a terrible blast took place. His small body was blown to bits. The ocean was full of mines, and so was the ground. The news of death, torture and tragedy became our daily portion for five years.

Burned-Earth Tactic

In the fall of 1944 the Germans began to leave our part of the country. As they left, they practiced the Burned-Earth tactic, which they had learned from the Russians. The Burned-Earth tactic was to burn what could be burned and utterly destroy the rest, so nothing would be left for the Russians. During the war we had no radio, as all radios had been confiscated right away. No newspaper existed, only German propaganda which was mostly in their favor. We were not sure what was going to take place. News was passed by word of mouth that the towns and villages east of us had been burned. For days we had seen the smoke rise to heaven, so we knew something was going on.

Friday night, November 3rd, my mother came from a prayer meeting. A little group of believers had met in a barn. She told us that the leader of that group had a dream. Jesus had come to him, holding a clock in his hand. The clock showed quarter to six. I will never forget November 5, 1944, my twelfth birthday. I did not undress nor would I let my little brother undress. We slept with clothes on. I woke up early in the morning, and walked over to Mom's and Dad's bedroom. "Should we not flee to the mountain today?" I asked. "You know Grandma is so slow to walk." (She was 86 years old.) As I was talking to them, I looked out the window and saw some warships approaching. At the same time a neighbor knocked on our door and told us the ships had come to burn. (The SS soldiers who came to burn and destroy were of a different caliber than the soldiers who stayed in the village during the war.) I asked Dad what time it was and he said, "A quarter to six." I remembered the dream, grabbed the hand of my little brother and we followed some neighbors who were running to the mountain.

We hid in a cleft of the mountain. Soon smoke from the village arose. Explosions and shooting started. My young heart was filled with sorrow and anguish as I wondered what was happening to the rest of the family. As I was praying for their safety, I watched the flames engulf our church. Orange flames licked eagerly over the old landmark. Soon the tower toppled over and the church bell made its last sound as it hit the ground. Many hours went by; we did not dare to move; we could not make a sound. A bullet flew over our heads and hit a sheep that was grazing above us. A neighbor came crawling toward us. He had foam around his mouth from crawling a long distance. I kept praying for my family, "Lord, be merciful; save their lives."

About one o'clock my mother came. I could not believe my eyes—here she was, the dearest of all my earthly possessions! Her coat and hair were scorched from the flames. Whispering she told us, "After you and your brother left, Dad and I started with Grandma. We were too slow, and soon the soldiers caught up with us. They demanded that we go with them to the ships. I said, 'No, I will not go with you. I have five children some place around here and I will not leave my children. You can shoot me if you wish, but I will not go with you unless the children are with me!'"

"'She is crazy,' one soldier said. 'Let her go.'"

So we learned that they took only my Dad and Grandma with them. Mom had walked the hot streets looking for us. Finally she found us. She almost collapsed from the nervous strain of losing track of her children, seeing her husband and mother-in-law taken prisoners, and watching the village burn and herself almost with it.

From the cleft we had a good view over the ocean; in the late afternoon we saw the warships departing. Their evil destruction had been accomplished.

Later my two brothers and sister found us. How glad we were that at least we had each other. On the other hand, we were awfully sad for Dad, Grandma and also the three older brothers who had left us earlier. What was their fate? Would we ever see them again?

We had not eaten all day, but now with the warships gone, we could move around a little bit. Some people found a goat, which they milked, and the bowl of goat milk was passed around, each getting a few sips. A couple of the men took the sheep that was shot earlier, butchered it and cut some chunks of meat from it. Soon these were cooking on a campstove in back of the crevice. With some broth and meat we were strengthened.

It was dark. The Polar Night had hid us. Time came to rest, but how could 23 people sleep in such a small place? They decided that the women and smaller children should rest at night, while the men and older boys kept watch. In this way we took turns.

I will never forget the first time I saw the village after it was burned. What a sight of total destruction. The main fire had burned down, and only the heaps of coals were glowing. People had stored their winter coal and now it burned like big campfires . . . some of it for months afterwards. The fishing vessels had been sunk and bridges blown up. Here we were—cut off from civilization, no telephones, no roads, no boats, no radios, no trees to cut down to rebuild. And that so far beyond the Arctic Circle, facing the Polar Night.

The Miracle That Saved Our Lives

All earthly hope seemed to fade, but there was One watching us with tender care. The Lord performed a miracle that year. If the weather had been as severe as usual, we all would have died within a short time. But the Lord held his hand of mercy over us—there was no snow and no wind. As we read in Mark 4:37-41, *"And there arose a great storm of wind, and the waves beat into the ship, so that it was now full. And he was in the hinder part of the ship, asleep on a pillow: and they awake him, and say unto him, Master, carest thou not that we perish? And he arose, and rebuked the wind, and said unto the sea, Peace, be still. And the wind ceased, and there was a great calm. And he said unto them, Why are ye so fearful? how is it that ye have no faith? And they feared exceedingly, and said one to another, What manner of man is this, that even the wind and the sea obey him?"*

Cave Survival And The Chilling Graveyard Experience

A few days later we moved into a cave that we found. The cave was about 21 steps underground. It had two entrances, so we could escape if one entrance was blocked. Inside, the cave had a number of rooms. We rigged up a stove, and at least we could bake bread. The main cooking was done in big washpots over the coal fires in the village. Bless his heart, Dad had dug down a few items when he heard the rumor of burning. Now we had some clothing and a couple of sacks of flour. We also found a supply of dried fish and still had some sheep to butcher. Our cow had escaped and provided us with milk. We loved that cow and did not want to kill her. Her name was "Dagros," which means "Dayrose." Now the big question was: where would we keep Dagros? for she needed shelter. We looked around and discovered that on the graveyard stood a thin board house. It was being used to keep people who died during the winter, until the frost melted away. Then they could dig graves and bury them. Luckily no one had died so far that fall and the house was empty. It became the home for Dagros.

I usually went milking with my Mom. She always sat on a gravestone as she milked. One evening as we were returning to the cave, Mother said, "Inger, I forgot a bucket in the graveyard. Will you please return and fetch it for me?" It was a little spooky as I entered the graveyard alone and looked for the bucket among the graves. The moon was shining, casting shadows of the crosses. Beyond the graveyard the campfires of coal were still glowing like a big mad monster with many eyes. I was glad when I caught up with Mother, and we returned to the cave.

One morning as we came to milk, Dagros had knocked out part of the wall, and was half inside, half outside. Apparently she did not like her new home and neighborhood. Without shelter, without food, we knew her life had come to an end.

The cave we lived in was inside the German fort. In fact, the soldiers had built the cave as a bomb shelter. Plenty of ammunition still lay around, and it was a temptation for the boys. They knew better than to play with some of it. There were *karduskas,* which looked like yellow wafers and burned with a fury. My brother Svein, 14, and his friend Kristian, 12, decided they would surprise their mothers. With a bunch of *karduskas* they went to the top of the cave and threw them into the stovepipe. Needless to say, the two poor ladies had the shock of their lives. Peacefully they were making bread; suddenly the stove started to roar, and they were engulfed in flames. The naughty sinners were caught, and some crying was heard. It did not happen again.

It was different living in a cave than in a house. With no windows we had to burn candles all the time. We made our own from sheep tallow.

One boy in our group needed pants badly. He was so ragged that some made a joke, saying to him, "Even St. Peter would not let you in if you should knock on the gate." The only thing we found to make pants from was an old blanket. It was folded in the middle (we had no pattern), and the boy was laid on the blanket. They cut around him. The pants were sewed by hand, and a drawstring inserted to hold them up. There is a great deal you can do when you have to do it.

We had one big problem, and that was to keep clean. Somehow lice got among us. Those nasty little things could really make life miserable for us. For years we were not able to get proper combs; we only had some crude ones made out of wood. They were not fine enough to catch the "critters." No lice powder or soap was available. We boiled the clothing and hung it for days out in the frost. To no avail; the lice still seemed to prosper. We had a council meeting and it was decided that all the children would have their hair shaved off, because it was a good place for our enemy to hide. Our barber arrived with his hand clippers and soon we looked like miniatures of Yul Brynner. One boy did not like what he saw and began to make a fuss. He was not going to be scalped. The barber comforted him and said, "I will just do a little trimming." Kristian relaxed, and boom, with the speed of a lightning bolt, the clippers made a clean cut right from his forehead to the back of his neck. What a sight he now was! The boy decided to have the rest also cut off.

Evacuation And Sardine-Style Living

One day we heard the good news, that one place farther east had not been burned. The authorities wanted to evacuate us to this place. The first ones to be moved were the sick, the old, and the families from which the men had been taken prisoners. That meant that we had to leave. We packed a few items, as not too much could be brought along. Mother insisted on taking Dagros along. She was now a barrel of salted meat. We needed food.

The night we left is graven in my mind. We had to travel in the dark with no light on the boat. The boat had orders to follow the shore as much as possible. If we hit a mine, or a submarine or ship tried to get us, we could run the boat ashore and escape. We were packed like sardines. I got seasick. I felt so miserable. How many hours the boat trip took I cannot recall. We were so thankful to the Lord when once again we could move about on dry ground.

We arrived at Båtsfjord. Its inhabitants shared the little they had with us refugees. We got one abode for us, mother's sister, and her daughter—eight people in one little room. Again we lived in sardine style. We made one big bed and all slept on it. During daytime, we rolled up the bed. This created living space. No wonder I get claustrophobia once in a while. It must be from my childhood experience. We lived like this for about six months. Our food supplies dwindled many a time, but God has a way, where there is no way. We ate whale and seal meat, sea gulls, codliver oil, dried fish, salt fish, wild birds' eggs and wild berries. My aunt, who also was a firm believer, joined my mother in prayer. The two dear saints fought many a battle on their knees. Often the question was asked, when will the war end, how much more will we have to suffer? Are Dad and Grandma still alive? What about my three brothers who had left home in their teens? The oldest one was working as a coast guard. The next one studied in Oslo. The third one had left home at age 15, to sail for the merchant marine. For months we did not hear a thing.

3

Peace, Freedom, Reunion and Reconstruction

Then the 8th of May, 1945, arrived. We were again a free people. The war was over. The joy is hard to describe. People dug into their attics to find the Norwegian flag. They ran into the streets, hugged each other, waved the flags, and sang the songs again which had been forbidden for over five long years. What a glorious feeling to be free! The country was war-torn, but the spirit of the people was loving, free and bold. Out of the ruins we rebuilt our country. Many had given their lives. Their sacrifice will never be forgotten.

A few days later we had another surprise. The first ship arrived from the south of Norway, and on that ship was my Dad. He had been waiting for a boat to bring him back home. How unbelievably good it was to see Dad again. Later that evening, as we were sitting really close to him, he told us what had happened after Mother left him and Grandma to look for us. Our eyes were glued to his lips as he spoke. "As we had to turn around to walk with the soldiers back to the warship, Grandma's eyes became dim as she saw the destruction. It was more than she could take, seeing her beloved village burn, and that she was a prisoner now. On the boat trip to the south she got sick. In a town called Tromsø I was able to get her to the hospital. A few days later she died.

"Later I was able to make it to my sister on the west coast of Norway. Her house was not bombed nor burned, so I stayed with her, waiting and hoping for an opportunity to make the trip north to look for you. But there were no boats going. Only when the war was over I could travel, and was happy to be on the first boat." He continued to tell us the good news, that our three oldest brothers were also alive. It was a miracle beyond a shadow of doubt. We had lost everything of our earthly possessions, but the best of all we had each other, and we were free, free, free!

Soon we left for our home town. It had no houses to dwell in, but army tents arrived. People came from every direction and temporarily lived in these tents. Shiploads of materials arrived, and people were building almost around the clock to get shelter for themselves before they would be facing winter again.

4
Teenage Years

By now I was a teenager, wondering about life as a whole: what was it all about?—what is to follow our earthly pilgrimage? I was so full of vim and vigor that I wanted the most out of life. I had seen God's provision and love during the dark years of war, so I looked to Christians to see if they had the answers —but they looked too old-fashioned and boring. They did not appeal to me.

I wanted to go dancing to see if that would satisfy my longing soul. I will never forget Mother's pleading not to go; but I was determined and went. As I danced, I thought, "Is this what they call fun?" Inside me something was crying as there was no peace. When I went to bed that night, I could not pray. I had always prayed before, but now I felt like a hypocrite, asking God to bless me and watch over me when I had gone my own worldly way and taken my life into my own hands. I struggled for years to find peace and happiness in the world, but there was none. I just fed on empty husks.

One night my girl friend asked me to go with her to a prayer meeting. I went mostly out of curiosity, but the power of the Lord was so strong in that meeting that I could not help but fall on my knees and call upon the Living God. What a wonderful experience! A joy and peace flooded my soul. Only those who have had the experience, know what I mean. I felt like an eagle soaring the high heavens after having been kept in a chicken coop for a long time. In Psalm 16:11 we read: *"Thou wilt shew me the path of life: in thy presence is fulness of joy; at thy right hand there are pleasures forevermore."* To follow the Master is not always an easy road, but there is joy in following Him.

The Christians I thought were so sober-minded and old-fashioned, became my best friends. They were a small group, not much to look at from the outside. The real beauty was inside. Like the Tabernacle in the wilderness, it was not much to look at from the outside as it was covered with goatskin. I am sure many an enemy from a foreign tribe climbed a mountain-top and spied the camp of the Israelites. They likely wondered about the building with the goat cover, so ugly and funny from the outside. They did not see the beauty inside—the gold, the curtains of blue, purple and scarlet, the mercy seat that covered the ark of the covenant and the candlesticks; the holy anointing oil, the pure incense of sweet spices, and the glory of the Lord that filled the Tabernacle.

5

Arrival in America—
My New Homeland

One summer my aunt and uncle came back to Norway from America for a visit. As we talked together, they wanted to know if I would like to visit the New World. "Oh, yes, " I said, "I would love to!" But America seemed so far away and I did not have any money, nor did I speak English. I wondered how it could come to pass. My aunt and uncle said they would lend me the money to pay for the trip over and take care of all the paper work that was necessary. They also said,

"Don't worry about the language; you will learn like the rest of us."

My Mother did not like the idea. She said, "They are so sinful over there and you may lose out with Almighty God." She quoted from Matthew 16:26: *"For what is a man profited, if he shall gain the whole world, and lose his own soul? or what shall a man give in exchange for his soul?"* However, my mind was made up to go. My Mother's pleading did not change it. When she saw that I was determined, she gave me a verse from the Bible and asked me to claim it as my very own: *"And the Lord, he it is that doth go before thee; he will be with thee, he will not fail thee, neither forsake thee: fear not, neither be dismayed."* (Deut. 31:8).

With this verse, a ticket bought with borrowed money, and four sentences of English, I waved goodbye to my little hometown of 450 people, where I knew every person, every house, and every street. All was left behind. Before me waited that great country . . . so unknown to me, yet drawing me so strongly.

Never will I forget my first glimpse of New York City as we anchored outside waiting for morning to dock. I looked at the lights—millions of them—and saw many automobiles rushing by. "Why this great hurry?" I wondered. Then I remembered how little English I spoke and that I was only on the East Coast of America. A long journey across the country still faced me. Sudden fear took hold of me—but then the verse my mother had given me popped into my mind . . . that the Lord had promised to go before me. I also remembered His faithfulness to the children of Israel. His Word says that He is the same yesterday, today and forever. As I meditated upon Him, peace flooded my soul and mind. It was so good to know that *the eternal God is our refuge, and underneath are the everlasting arms.* (Deut. 33:27).

The next day, just as I was about to leave the ship, I heard my name called over the loudspeaker. At the ship's office they told me another young lady aboard was also going to Seattle and wanted to travel with me. Her aunt would shortly pick us up and take us to the airport. That aunt could speak both English and Norwegian. She showed us part of New York City, bought lunch and helped us find the right airplane. My heart greatly rejoiced as I realized the Lord's provision. The flight went smoothly. My aunt and uncle met me in Seattle. It was such a joy to see them again!

They drove me over to meet my brother Paul, who had left home at the age of fifteen to sail for the merchant marine just before the Second World War started. I could barely remember him as I was only seven when he left. Paul was now married and had five children. As we were talking, I asked him how he escaped the war. Then he said, "I was on a boat, and we were sailing to South America. I got very sick, and had to go to the hospital."

"What happened to the ship after you left?" I asked.

"No one knows," he said, "it was never heard from again. Apparently it hit a mine, or was torpedoed."

After Paul got well, he wrote to his two aunts in the U.S.A. They sponsored him as an immigrant into America. As I listened to his story, I was again reminded of God's answer to prayer, and His faithfulness. Mother and her sister had united in prayer for days, claiming the Scripture *". . . That if two of you shall agree on earth as touching any thing that they shall ask, it shall be done . . ."* (Matt. 18:19).

As I now viewed my new country, how impressed I was with the beautiful flowers, delicious-looking vegetables and super-markets filled with food! "This is just like paradise; people must be happy," I thought. But I was surprised to see the empty, hurried look on so many faces. Another thing that really puzzled me, was the attitude people took when you visited them while they were watching their favorite television pro-grams. You could hardly squeeze in "How are you?" while the commercial was on! In Norway we had time to talk with each other and be concerned one for another. When you asked, "How are you?" you really meant it. And you wanted to know about aches, pains and all.

I went to work for a family with four girls. My job was to be their "nanny." The girls were very good to me and tried very hard to teach me English. In the playroom they would take their teddy bear, point to the nose, and say "nose," point to the eyes, and say "eyes." So, little by little I was learning my new language.

6
Falling in Love

One day someone told me about a church in downtown Seattle that held Norwegian services every Sunday afternoon. How wonderful it was to go there and sing the good, old-fashioned songs again and hear the gospel preached in my own language! It satisfied my soul. At one meeting my girl friend whispered, "Look to your left and see the nice fellow sitting next to you. He is a bachelor." I looked. Yes, it was true, he was a very nice-looking man.

After the meeting we had refreshments downstairs. I was introduced to Sigvart Wathne who had been sitting beside me during the meeting. He was tall and had blue eyes, blond hair and a very pleasant smile. Later, he asked if he could drive me home. I said, "Yes." The next day my girl friend called me and said, "I hope you did not fall in love with Sig. He is nice and a clean-cut fellow. He takes out all the newly-arrived girls but has not married any of them. So don't fall in love with him—you will only be brokenhearted."

I took her advice. Sig and I saw each other when I had a day off. We were good friends. We enjoyed talking with each other and about our wonderful Saviour Jesus Christ. One night as we were talking, he said, "I am tired of being a bachelor. I would like to get married." "Why don't you?" I said. "You know so many girls, it should not be hard to pick one from among so many."

"Would *you* marry me?" he asked. My heart jumped! I had liked him very much from the moment we first met, but when my girl friend told me not to fall in love with him, I always kept that in mind and did not allow myself to care for him beyond the basis of friendship. As we asked our Heavenly Father for His will in this matter, we sensed a peace and a "go-ahead" from Him. Shortly afterward we were married in the same church where we had first met.

What a new world opened up! Oh, it is beyond description to be married to the one whom you love so much!

A Comical Misunderstanding

Sig and I decided that we did not want a TV in our home. No, we wanted to talk together instead of watching the boob tube. One program, however, he liked to see was "The $64,000 Question." So sometimes we were tempted to buy one.

One day after Sig had just left for work, the doorbell rang and I opened the door. A man stood in the doorway, smiled, and said, "Would you like a T.B. x-ray for your chest?" Since I had only been in America a short time, my English was not too good. I thought he asked if I wanted to buy a TV, so I said, "You see, I am newly married. My husband and I want to talk together; we don't want a TV."

The man looked at me strangely, and said, "A T.B. x-ray for your chest."

"Yes, I understand what you mean. You want to sell us a portable one since you say chest." By now I could see he was getting impatient.

"Lady, it is free; come with me," he said.

Free! that was unbelievable. I hesitated for a moment; what would my husband say? Then I ran after the man. One doesn't get a free TV every day.

We went down the stairway, and then walked one block to a van. The man pushed me against an apparatus and said, "Take a deep breath." Suddenly it dawned on me what he was trying to tell me. As I walked home, I got the giggles—I had to laugh and laugh.

7

Bundles of Joy

A year after we were married, our first baby was born. When I looked into our little son's deep blue eyes, I could see heaven. The look Roy gave me was so cute, so trusting, like an angel. My happiness as a brand new mother knew no limit—I wept for joy. It was as if the whole creation rejoiced with me this 2nd of March, 1958, a Sunday morning.

Through my open window I heard the church bell ringing, and the birds singing. Right outside the window was a Japanese cherry tree in full bloom; then it started to snow lightly. Big white flakes came sailing down ever so slowly. It was like spring and winter having a tug of war. Did the snow have a message?

About two-and-a-half years later Tom arrived. "Another truck driver," a proud daddy announced. He did not seem disappointed at all, although he had hoped for a girl to be next. I did not care, boy or girl, as long as the baby was normal and healthy.

The Red Fury Devours Our Mansion

Now with two boys the upstairs apartment seemed too small, and so we decided to build a house in the north end of Edmonds. It was a happy day when we moved into our new home with a lovely view of Puget Sound and the snowcapped mountains of the Olympic National Park. We imported furniture from Norway, had wall-to-wall wool carpets in the living and dining rooms, and the draperies custom-made. It was the first time in my life that I lived in a pretty place. I began to watch if people walked on my carpet with dirty shoes, and if the children had clean hands that touched the furniture. I was carried away and began to adore the house.

Then one night, about seven weeks after we moved into the house, we discovered it was on fire! Only by the grace of God were we able to escape with our lives! As we stood there, looking at all our work and plans going up in flames, my first thought was, "God, You must do something! Can't you stop the fire?" But I had to bow my head in shame. He is Alpha and Omega, the beginning and the end. He knows what is best for His children. I whispered, "Lord, Thy will be done." A sweet peace and rest came over me.

I realized my eyes had been on the house—now the Lord wanted to give me a better view. In John 14:2 we read: *"In my Father's house are many mansions; if it were not so, I would have told you. I go to prepare a place for you."* I had forgotten the place He was preparing for me. My desires and thoughts had been so earthbound. Jesus says in Matthew 6:20, 21: *"But lay up for yourselves treasures in heaven, where neither moth nor rust doth corrupt, and where thieves do not break through nor steal; For where your treasure is, there will your heart be also."* There is nothing wrong with having a nice home, but it should not come ahead of Jesus Christ. He must come first.

We read in Matthew 17:1-8 about Jesus taking His disciples Peter, James and John up on a high mountain. They had the wonderful experience of seeing Jesus transfigured in front of them and of hearing Him talking to Moses and Elijah. Peter got all excited and said to Jesus, *". . . Lord, it is good for us to be here: if thou wilt, let us make here three tabernacles; one for thee, and one for Moses, and one for Elias. While he yet spake, behold, a bright cloud overshadowed them: and behold a voice out of the cloud, which said, This is my beloved Son, in whom I am well pleased; hear ye him. And when the disciples heard it, they fell on their face, and were sore afraid. Jesus came and touched them, and said, Arise, and be not afraid. And when they had lifted up their eyes, they saw no man, save Jesus only"* (Matt. 17:4-8). Yes, He must be our all in all. I love the hymn that contains these words:

"Turn your eyes upon Jesus,
Look full in His wonderful face,
And the things of earth will grow strangely dim
In the light of His glory and grace."

As I talked to one of the firemen afterward, he said to me, "Sorry about your home, lady." I looked at him and said, "Be not sorry—my real home is in heaven and nothing can destroy it. The things we have on earth are so vulnerable; today we have them, tomorrow they can be gone. Our only safety is in Jesus."

The fireman shook his head; he did not say any more. I guess he was thinking, "That poor woman has not only lost her home, but she also lost a few marbles along with it."

The house was a sad sight after the fire was extinguished, but in my heart was a joy that only Christ can give. We had insurance, so the house was rebuilt. It was now the Lord's house, and I just thanked Him for letting me live there.

Soon after the fire, Helen came on the scene. Finally, finally, the girl had arrived that her Daddy had talked about for so long. He always wanted a baby girl. Now she had come, and he was very pleased. There is something sweet about a baby, each one so unique and precious, each one so dear to your heart. You love them so dearly and you are willing to die for them any day if you must.

Not By Feeling But By Faith

I can well remember the day, as I was nursing Helen, when the boys played next to me. I was meditating upon the Lord and it seemed that He was so far off. I took the Bible and opened it up and began to read in Isaiah 49:14-16, *"But Zion said, The Lord hath forsaken me, and my Lord hath forgotten me. Can a woman forget her sucking child, that she should not have compassion on the son of her womb? yea, they may forget, yet will not I forget thee. Behold, I have graven thee upon the palms of my hands; thy walls are continually before me."*

How sweet of the Lord to talk to me in a language I well knew. Being a mother, I understood what He meant. So often in our Christian walk we go by feeling, not by the Word of God. I am an American citizen, not by birth but by choice. I do not always feel like an American, especially when it comes to spelling and history. But if I doubt, I can always open my drawer and look at the naturalization certificate which states that I am a citizen. So it is with my heavenly citizenship. I am a child of God no matter how I feel. I often failed God, but He has never failed me.

8

Suddenly Death Strikes

On April 20th, 1964, I could hardly wait until Roy left for kindergarten. I put Helen and Tom down for naps. I was so tired—if I could only sleep! The two little ones came down with mumps and I had been up for several nights with them. Now the house was quiet and I finally rested. I fell asleep right away, and had a dream. I saw an angel sealing off our lot around the house. I asked him what he was doing? He looked at me and said, "From now on this property is under my care."

I woke up as Roy came back from school. He said, "Mommy, Mommy! Something has happened where Daddy works! When I went by on the school bus, I saw the ambulance and the police in the gravel pit!"

I rushed to the telephone and called. "Yes," they said, "there has been an accident and your husband is buried. The gravel bank he was digging from has caved in and we are trying to find him." So many thoughts whirled through my mind as anxiety gripped my heart. "Lord, be merciful! Oh, let him live! Please let him live!" But it was as though my prayer froze on the ceiling and dripped down icily on my back. Finally, I cried out, "Lord, Thy will be done!" Then it was as though heaven opened up. Oh, the comfort that only He can give to a broken and sorrowing heart!

A little later the minister arrived with the news that my husband was dead. We prayed together and other friends came and joined in prayer. Kind and comforting words were spoken. It was so hard to find the right expressions in such a situation.

After everyone had gone home, the house seemed so empty. I remembered what the minister had said on the "happy day" Sig and I got married. He proclaimed, "The two of you shall be one." Truly, we were one, but now Sig was dead. I felt like an empty shell.

How about the children, could I bring them up alone? I did not have an answer to all the questions that came to my mind, so I took my Bible and asked the Lord to give me a verse to hang onto. As I opened my Bible, my eyes fell on Isaiah 54. There were many verses in that chapter and it seemed as though they were written just for me. In verse five I read, *"For thy Maker is thine husband; the Lord of hosts is his name; . . ."* What a promise! He was not only my Saviour, but He was also my husband now! In verse ten the Lord says, *"For the mountains shall depart, and the hills be removed; but my kindness shall not depart from thee, neither shall the covenant of my peace be removed, saith the Lord that hath mercy on thee."* How I loved verse 13: *"And all thy children shall be taught of the Lord; and great shall be the peace of thy children."*

Tears streamed down my face as I realized that He was going with me through my sorrow. He was a man of sorrows and acquainted with grief. But in spite of the sorrow and lonely hours there was a peace and a nearness of Him that said, *"I will never leave you nor forsake you."* How great is His faithfulness!

A Song In The Night

About three weeks after Sig had died I felt especially lonely. It was one of those nights when the sky was so gray, and the rain poured and poured. The children were tucked in bed, and the house was ever so quiet. The loss of my companion just overwhelmed me. "Oh, Lord," I cried, "it would not be so bad if You only had given me a chance to say good-bye to him. But You took him home so suddenly."

That night, I had a comforting dream. In it Sig came to me dressed in a long gown. The gown was not only white, but dazzling white. On his face was the biggest smile, and he said to me, "Inger, I can sing; do you want me to sing for you?" So he sang. I cannot recall the song. It was beyond description. The voice was ever so full and harmonic. Never on Earth had I heard anything so beautiful. Then the dream faded.

I woke up, got out of bed and walked to the kitchen. As I looked out the window I saw Sig's identical twin brother Henry walk to the gravel truck dressed in his gray coveralls. My dream came to mind—what a different picture! Sig so happy, dressed in white being able to sing. To sing had always been his dream. Since he could not carry a tune, he wanted to marry a girl who could sing and play the guitar. When he married me, that dream was crushed, too. My brothers used to tell me when I was little, "Inger, if your voice belonged to a goat, we could not eat the meat nor drink the milk." I was unable to carry a tune, not even in a bucket. Musically, he had not gained anything by marrying me. But now his dream had come true. He could sing for his Lord and Master.

A few weeks later someone gave me a book to read. It was written by Catherine Marshall, and I believe the name of the book was *To Live Again*. She also lost her husband. God gave her a dream in which she saw her husband working among roses. It was very comforting to her as well, because she knew how much her Peter liked roses.

A Hard Request With A Promise

One night as I was reading my Bible, I came upon Ephesians 5:20: *"Giving thanks always for all things unto God and the Father in the name of our Lord Jesus Christ."* It was just as though the Lord asked me, "Have you given Me thanks for taking your husband?"

"Lord, You don't mean that!" I said aloud. I read the verse again: "Giving thanks always for *all* things . . ."—not just saying "thank you" when someone gives you a present or when the Lord trusts you with a healthy baby, but saying "thank you" for the dark hours as well as the sunny hours He sends along our pathway. I knew I could not do it in my own strength. I knelt down in prayer and, when I asked Him for help, I was able to do it. Then the verse came to me: *"And we know that all things work together for good to them that love God, to them who are the called according to His purpose"* (Rom. 8:28).

The Wahtne family. From left to right, Roy, Inger, Sigvart with Helen on his lap, and Tom

9

Experiencing the Great Comforter Through Widowhood

As a widow I had many testings, but also many wonderful answers to prayer.

Orchids

How well I remember the first Mother's Day. I was sure there was not going to be any orchid. Sig had always bought me a beautiful corsage for this lovely occasion. But this day the Lord had a surprise for me. In the evening I not only had one orchid, but two! One I received in the morning from the children, bought by Aunt Louise and Uncle Henry. Later on the same day I was handed one for being the youngest mother in church. As I looked upon those lovely flowers, I bowed my head in shame. Here I had been so sure that there would be no flowers, and now the Lord had given me two. I remembered Isaiah 54:5: *"For thy Maker is thine husband; the Lord of hosts is His name . . ."* All I could say was "Thank you, Maker and husband."

The Lord's Protection

Our house was on a dead-end road. The road terminated about 50 yards farther down from our driveway. The other end of the street ran into a busy highway. Right here was a tavern. There they featured topless dancers which drew crowds. Sometimes at night the customers would take a wrong turn and get stuck in the mud where our street stopped. Occasionally they needed help to get out. Frequently the neighbors asked me, "Aren't you afraid to sleep alone with the children?"

I had to answer, "No, I am not afraid."

One night about 2 A.M. the phone rang. On the phone was Elinor, my neighbor. She said, "There is a car stuck in the mud, and a man is walking toward your property."

"Thank you, Elinor, for letting me know," I answered, half asleep, and hung up the phone. I went right back to sleep. As I was doing dishes next morning, I thought, "Didn't the phone ring last night, or was it a dream?"

I phoned Elinor to ask her if she had given me a ring last night. "Yes," she said, "I called you."

"Well, what happened to the man?"

"He walked right toward your house, but when he came to your property line, he turned around and left."

I remembered the dream I had the day Sig had died. The angel said, "From now on this property is under my care."

Car Trouble And The Lord's Mechanic

As a woman alone with children, I had to get away once in a while. During the winter I would go skiing for a day, and in the summer fishing. Both sports I love a lot.

As a family we enjoyed camping. We bought a tent and some sleeping bags, and soon the boys knew how to put up the tent in a jiffy. Helen would gather sticks for the campfire. The outdoor life was great.

I also went once a week to Bible study. One night as the class ended, I could not get the car started. I tried and tried to no avail. It was getting late, and I had promised the babysitter to be home by 9:30 P.M., and now it was almost 10 P.M. I looked around. There was only one car left on the parking lot besides me. I stepped out of the car; what could be wrong? It was dark and I had to splash with both feet into a puddle. Soon I was cold and wet. It was raining. A helpless and lonely feeling overcame me. "Dear Lord," I prayed, "here I am again. I don't know what to do, I must get home. Please, Lord, help me.

Remember You promised to be my husband, and Father for my children." I had not even finished praying when the last car on the parking lot started up and came driving toward me. He opened his car door and asked,

"Lady, what is your trouble?" So I told him. "Well," he said, "I am a car mechanic. Let us see what we can do." He opened the hood and worked awhile, and soon the car started. I was so happy.

"Thank you, Lord, thank you," I said.

"You know, it is strange," the man said, "I should have driven home long ago, but somehow I got so delayed, I just did not seem to be able to leave."

I told him about my prayer, and how I believed the Lord delayed him so he could help me.

Accidental Prisoners And The Locksmith

The Lord truly was a father for the fatherless as He has promised in His word. One day the children had locked themselves into the bathroom in a friend's house and we tried everything except breaking the door to get them out. I walked around the house to see if the bathroom had a window through which we could rescue them. There was no window. As I returned to the house, a man crossed my path. He looked at me and asked, "What is your trouble lady?"

"My children have locked themselves into the bathroom and I don't know how to get them out," I answered. He smiled and said,

"That is no trouble, you see, for I happen to be a locksmith."

I called upon the Lord for help and He sent a locksmith right to the door! Truly, the Lord performed many other wonderful miracles.

However, in spite of the Lord's goodness to us, I missed a companion. As we had our devotions, we prayed to God for a husband and father. We claimed Psalms 37:4, 5 as our promise from the Lord: *"Delight thyself also in the Lord; and he shall give thee the desires of thine heart. Commit thy way unto the Lord; trust also in him; and he shall bring it to pass."* He did!

10

My New Sweetheart—
Love Smiles Again

A few years later, in the summer of 1967, I was working at a Christian conference center in the Pacific Northwest. There I met Hans J. Schneider, a world-wide evangelist. He was the speaker one week. While having breakfast at the same table one day, we began to talk with each other and discovered many common interests. Both of us had seen war and all the terror that goes with it (Hans came from East Germany and had lived under a Communistic regime for five years).

We fell in love, but before anything was talked over, we both prayed and asked God for His will for our lives. Hans had to go back to Salem, Oregon, and I traveled back to Edmonds, Washington, to get the children started in school. Many letters and telephone calls were exchanged. Our love grew deep for each other, and the Lord's blessing was upon it, so we decided to get married.

On October 7, 1967, at 7:00 o'clock in the evening (seven being God's perfect number), we were joined together as husband and wife. I could say with David in Psalm 30:11, 12: *"Thou hast turned for me my mourning into dancing: thou hast put off my sackcloth, and girded me with gladness: To the end that my glory may sing praise to thee, and not be silent. O Lord my God, I will give thanks unto thee for ever."*

Both Hans and I had a burning desire to serve the Lord. He had been an evangelist for many years. And the Lord began to use me in sharing my testimony for ladies' groups and young people's services. Many said that they had been blessed. Often I was asked to write my story. Now we could combine our talents for the Lord.

One thing, we both agreed, was never to ask for money. We were serving a rich Heavenly Father, and we did not need to beg. It is heart-breaking to see how often in a service people are pressed into giving. Oh, how the spirit of the Lord is grieved by a money campaign. If we could not make it, we would do like Paul of old, work with our hands.

I sold my house in Edmonds, and moved to Salem where Hans had been living. One of our bedrooms was used as an office. We bought Bibles, New Testaments, and Gospels of John, Luke, Mark and Matthew and also had some Christian books to give away. Let me not forget to tell you about all the Bible tracts. We had several hundred different kinds. Literature was sent out free of charge to many missionaries and Christians in foreign countries. In the winter, when the children were in school, we wrote letters and sent out packages. It was a very rewarding work.

11

Evangelistic Tours and Wilderness Experiences

Summer On Wheels

As soon as school was out, we packed our Volkswagen camper and started our summer on wheels. I had not really seen much of America. My husband said we could make a combination missionary-national parks journey. Spectacular hikes through God's great country refueled our spiritual batteries.

One day, while hiking up Mt. Whitney, we learned some wonderful spiritual lessons. The higher we climbed, the more narrow, steep and rocky the trail became. Just as in our spiritual walk we encounter more difficulties and trials the closer we get to Christ. But the climb was well worth the effort, for, oh, what a wonderful view there was on top of that mountain!

When we came to towns and villages, we distributed Bible tracts. I will never forget a small town in Arizona where we handed out some of them. A man came running to us and asked, "Are you the parents of the little boys who gave out Bible tracts?" We said, "Yes." "You know, I read the tract and got so blessed. I am a Christian, too," he said.

"Now let us pray." Right there and then on a street corner we had a prayer meeting. He was so happy, he hugged us all and thanked God for sending us his way.

And so it was, never knowing, never planning for the next day, only moving from day to day as the good Lord led us. At night we slept outside on the ground; it was so heart-moving to lie out in the open, looking into a starry sky, close to God and happy in His presence.

The trip lasted for 103 days. We had hiked more than 500 miles. What an education for all of us!

Summer On Wings

My husband is a pilot. In 1969 we rejoiced to see our Heavenly Father provide a plane in a miraculous way. At the end of May we started our 96-day "summer family journey on wings." What wonderful experiences we had, as we looked out upon God's great country from above. It seems as though you can understand the Lord better when you look down upon His creation. Often in life we get puzzled and we don't have the answers to our problems. But one glorious day He will give us the upper view. Then we will see and understand that the dark threads were just as necessary as the threads of gold and silver in the pattern He planned.

Almost daily we visited with God's pearls all over the country and preached the wonderful Gospel of the kingdom of God.

Once we flew from Dallas, Texas, to Carlsbad Caverns, New Mexico. My husband was the speaker for the evening service. The weather was not the best when we started out, but the weatherman said it would improve during the day. It was cloudy with some breaks in the sky. We picked the biggest opening and circled around in it to gain altitude and get above the clouds. Soon we were on top, and enjoyed the lovely sunshine. Below us glistened the clouds, ever so pure and white. It reminded me of my childhood when we brought the sheep home from their summer pasture. Mom sheared them and we had a heap of white wool lying there.

We had not been flying long before we noticed a cloud layer above us. Soon we were sandwiched between two layers. I did not like it—it was too much for my claustrophobia. There was no choice but to continue. We were flying strictly by compass. Hours passed by and I was really praying that we would soon hit a cloudhole so we could descend. But no, we did not see any. I watched the gas gauge, and it was extremely low. We also needed to visit the restrooms. (I have often said, "I wonder what has the longest range, the gas tank or our bladders!")

Finally, we saw an opening and down we went. How good it was to see old Earth again! Our little bird was not too far from the airport. We called the pastor right away, and he came to pick us up. He drove us right to church. As we walked in, the people sang: "It Is Just Like Jesus To Roll The Clouds Away." Goose pimples formed on my skin. How could they know about the weather we had been flying in? We had not mentioned anything about it. The song really warmed my heart, because Jesus had answered my prayers that day, and rolled the clouds away.

There were many other highlights on this trip, such as visiting some of the islands in the Caribbean Sea. The blue-green waters showed occasional sharks in them as we flew overhead. We also saw Apollo 11 taking off right in front of us. Once we had just left the southeastern part of the U.S. when a mighty hurricane struck that area and made havoc of it.

Josef

We were in Tulsa, Oklahoma, on our westward journey back home. After 90 days of flying from place to place, never knowing what the next day would bring, it was good to return. But truly, it had been a very interesting summer.

I looked around in our small hotel room. My husband was busy with the maps, figuring out the best flying route. The children were outside playing. I knew I had to be quiet as Hans did not want to be disturbed with the map work. So I started to meditate upon the idea that perhaps we would be blessed with another baby. "Will it be a boy or a girl?" I wondered. Like lightning the answer came. "It's a boy!" I was stunned. A boy! What would we name him? "Josef."

"But, Lord, I don't like 'Josef,' it sounds so old-fashioned. How about Peter, John, Philip or Andrew?"

It was no use. As soon as I could think of a name, it would be blotted out. It was just like a blackboard inside me. I was writing names that I liked on it, and someone with a big sponge was erasing them. This was a game I had never played before. Then the name Josef came with such firmness, I did not dare to argue. This had never happened to me. I did not say a word to my husband. He would not believe me, anyhow. He might just smile and say, "But, sweetheart, your imagination is playing a trick with you."

Our friends then came and took us on a sight-seeing trip through Tulsa. What a great day we spent with them. In the evening, we went to a hamburger stand for a bite to eat, and after the meal we said good-bye to our friends. They wanted to take us to our hotel room, but we said, "It is only a few blocks away and we need the exercise." So we walked. It was a lovely evening with a dark blue sky laced with stars. Suddenly my husband turned to me and said, "We will call him Josef."

"Why Josef?" I asked, "Please tell me." I could feel the goose pimples all over my skin. This was strange indeed. So he told me word for word what I had experienced that same morning. He did not like 'Josef' either and had argued the point, but to no avail. The Lord let him as well know that the boy's name was Josef.

On the 19th of April, 1970, Josef John arrived—in spite of the assurance of the doctor that it would be a girl.

Alaskan Adventure

In 1970 we spread our wings again, this time to Canada and Alaska, where my husband conducted about a dozen meetings in such places as Fairbanks, Anchorage, Nome, and Petersburg. People there were so heartwarming and real. They seemed to be hungry for more of God. We had great fellowship with them.

We seldom make up any schedule or arrangements as we travel—we just go from day to day as the good Lord leads. What an interesting way of life: When He wanted us to stay, the sky was closed; when He wanted us to move on, the weather cleared up. Seeing the overwhelming scenery of that northern country with its crisp, clear air, multitudes of lakes, glaciers reaching all the way down to sea level and gigantic mountains all over, gave us a new and unforgettable understanding of how great the One who made all this must be, and to know this One is the supreme thing in our lives.

In the Yukon we tried panning gold. We thanked God that our riches are in Christ Jesus as we read the story of the great gold rush and all the hardships the people endured, with only a few striking it rich. How much more fervent should we be who have found Jesus Christ as our Saviour, and to tell others about Him should be our greatest joy.

It was different to travel with a small baby. As always, we brought our camping gear along. Now I also had a stack of diapers. Food for the baby was no problem, because I was nursing him. Josef seemed to be born to fly. He enjoyed it so much. We often landed on small airports, where we normally inquired if it was all right to camp. Then we pitched our pup tent, got our campstove going, and made a warm meal. Afterwards, we usually put the baby in the Jerry-pack and went exploring. I remembered that once a man said, "You better not camp here. I don't think it is safe. Last night we had three bears raiding the garbage can."

Once we flew along the ocean and spotted a school of giant whales that had the time of their lives playing in the ocean. They chased each other, diving below and jumping above the sea, while blowing water fountains into the air. My husband circled lower and lower. We were all so fascinated by their game.

At this point, let me quote what my husband states so well about the remainder of our Alaskan trip on pages 223–224 in his book *Flying to Be Free* (available from World Wide Publishing Corporation, P.O. Box 105, Ashland, OR 97520-0105):

". . . on our return trip from Juneau to Petersburg, Alaska, we encountered very bad weather and flew at times 66 feet over the sea. After a lovely visit with some nice friends, we decided to fly the coast all the way to the conterminous USA. We made a short stopover in Annette, Alaska, after an 80-minute trip in order to fuel up the plane and get the latest weather reports. A long journey awaited us.

"Here flight service issued strong warnings against travelling this way VFR with a small, single-engine aircraft. 'Just the other day we heard an SOS from a pilot cruising along the coast nearby. Extremely bad weather made it impossible to rush to his help immediately. It can change here very quickly for the worse. All we found of him, days later, was an empty gas container floating in the ocean. We never traced him nor his plane. Along this stretch we usually have only one day of good weather per year—that is, sufficiently good for your type of aircraft. We are losing planes here all the time. It's one of the worst routes!'

"That was quite a consolation. In spite of the warning, we went ahead as planned. The coastline was rugged. The shore dropped off as mountains met the sea, and there was no place for an emergency landing. To make it yet more exciting, the engine developed roughness south of Prince Rupert, Canada. 'What if the motor quits at this time?' I comforted my wife. Otherwise, it was a nice day. No clouds, and beautiful weather most of the way. But from the middle of Vancouver Island it started to get hazy. So-called "blessings" of civilization that far north! Then finally, after a six-hour flight, we reached Snohomish County Paine Field near Seattle, Washington. A month of challenging experiences in Canada and Alaska lay behind us."

Grounded By A Rose

After two marvellous summers of flight, I was now grounded. The reason: Another baby was due in August. Receiving Josef's name right away by inspiration rather spoiled us. We somehow expected the same thing to happen again, but it did not. What name to pick was the big question. "You know," I said to my husband, "as we read in the Bible about Josef, it says that Josef's little brother was named Benjamin. Why not call him Benjamin?"

"No," said my husband. "I don't like Benjamin because Rachel died when she gave birth to Benjamin, and I don't want you to die." Soon we understood why we couldn't decide on another boy's name, because a girl arrived. We finally decided on Rose Sharon, found in the Song of Solomon 2:1.

And truly a Rose appeared on the 17th of August, 1971. She was such a pretty baby with dark blue eyes and dark hair. She looked as if she spent her last few days on the French Riviera obtaining a lovely suntan. "She looks like an Indian," my husband said. We all enjoyed our new baby so much. The older children fought over her—she was just like a doll. Josef John did not say much about her, for he was only 16 months old. He was still a baby, too, and needed a great deal of love and care.

When Rose was two months old, my husband and Roy criss-crossed America by plane on a nine-month speaking tour. They had about 400 meetings. Tom and Helen were going to school, and I was home caring for the babies, packing packages and writing letters. Many requests came from the mission field. I received letters from Ghana, Nigeria, Indonesia, India, Cameroon, New Zealand, Australia and many other places. Some of the letters were so cute. One wrote: "Please send us a Bible, our eyes will be in the mailbox." It was a busy, but happy time.

One lesson we learned that winter was, if you take a stand for the Lord and honor Him, He will back you up and help you. As a family we always had our devotions. We studied the Word of God with the children. Our home did not have any television, nor would we dress according to this world's fashion.

When you take a stand for the Lord, it is not always easy. Helen at times came home from school crying. Some of the boys had pulled her hair, and called her 'grandma,' because she did not wear mini-skirts. Finally, one day I had enough. "Helen," I said, "let us really pray about it. God is able to take care of it." We prayed. I reminded God that we were working for Him, that we needed His help in this situation. A few days later she came home all smiles. "What happened?" I asked.

"Everything is fine," she said. "The boys that used to be mean to me are not on the bus anymore; they moved away."

I could hardly believe what she told me. "Let us go and see," I said. "It's time to take the babies for a walk anyway." So we hiked and looked at their homes, and all three homes had

"For Sale" signs. God had moved them away. What a lesson it was for me and especially for the children to see how God can help us in every situation.

Arriving home from an evangelistic tour, young Roy and Hans alight from the family plane to greet Inger (holding baby Rose), little Josef, Helen, and Tom

12
My Bout With Cancer

The first part of 1972 I did not feel good. I don't know how to explain it. There was no pain any place and it just felt as if all the strength had left me. When my husband called home, I told him how I felt.

"You better have a real good checkup," he said. I went to see a doctor and had a complete physical. He asked me to fill out a questionnaire about my family history and return the next week for the results. At the next appointment he told me, "The only thing we could find wrong is that you are anemic." He gave me some iron pills and sent me home. As I left, my heart was crying. I knew within myself that something was desperately wrong, but what?

When my husband called again, I reported to him what the doctor had said.

"Listen, Inger, I want you to take Rose and fly down to Dallas, Texas. Roy and I will meet you there. Get a babysitter for the other children. I think that it is very important for you to have a checkup with Dr. Kelley." Hans continued, "I definitely feel that the Lord has led us to this missionary couple we are staying with in Florida. The lady of the house had stomach cancer and had to leave the mission field. Now she is being treated by Dr. Kelley along natural lines, and she is doing fine."

Rose and I flew on a big airliner, so different from our Cessna. When we arrived, Hans and Roy met us. It was so good to see them! I had not been with them for about six months.

The next day Hans, Roy and I had a blood test taken by Dr. Kelley. We waited about three hours for the results. I will never forget what happened when we were seated in the office. Dr. Kelley looked very serious, as he began to talk.

"Mr. Schneider, your test came out fine, also Roy's; but Mrs. Schneider has cancer on her small intestines and in her left breast, weighing about one pound together. The situation is very serious and she must start the treatment immediately."

Cancer! The word stuck in my mind. "Inger, you got cancer," I whispered to myself. Cancer was something that happened to other people; but now it had me as a victim. I peeked at little Rose in my arms; she looked so trusting. Little did she understand. My eyes glanced at Hans and Roy; and how about the children at home—what would they say to this?

When we returned to the motel, I said to my husband, "Would you be so kind to watch Rose; I must go for a hike; I need to be alone."

As I was hiking along, I looked down on the dark, gray gravel road that matched my mood. My world had crumbled and I was going to die, all the people I had known that got cancer died. Now my turn had come. But when we are in despair, Jesus is ever so near. It seemed as if He said, "Inger, look up." As I did, I realized what a glorious spring day it was.

I had left the city and was now hiking in the country along a fence. Horses were grazing inside the fence, a colt was playing happily, bees and bumblebees kissed each flower, birds sang in the trees, while busily building their nests. The sky was ever so blue; it was like a giant sermon preached right before me: an invitation for me to live. How could I feel like dying when the whole creation was buzzing with life? "Oh, Lord, thank You for Your sermon," I said. "By Your grace I will live." New hope had come to me.

It took me about one year to get rid of the cancer. I was really bad off; the doctor told me later that he never thought I would pull through. I will not go into detail about the treatment, for it would make the book too lengthy. Perhaps, one day I will write a book about my struggle against cancer.

13

How We Found Shangri-La

For a few months we had been looking for acreage with a house on it. We needed space to grow a garden and have livestock. Helen intensely loved animals. She usually hugged each dog and cat she could lay her hands on. She would fall into daydreams when she saw a horse. So we contacted the local real estate broker. The more we looked, the more discouraged we became. It seemed as if there was something wrong with each place.

One day my husband said, "I will take the plane and search for land from above." He started in North-Eastern Oregon and was on his way to Cave Junction when the weather turned sour. In no way could he continue. So he set the bird down in Medford, Oregon, and began to call the different real estate outfits. United Farm Agency in Ashland indicated that they thought they might have what he was looking for. So they picked him up at the airport and drove him to Shangri-La. My husband was extremely happy with what he saw. Finally, his search had come to an end. All he had to do now was to fly home, pick up his honey baby and the children and show them their new home.

The next morning we left early, heading for the nearest airport to our destination, which was in Ashland. But first we flew over Shangri-La to study it from the air. I could hardly believe my eyes when I saw that lonely place tucked away among the trees. We kept circling; soon the babies in the back seat started to throw up, and Tom had his hands full trying to help them.

We then flew to the airport and landed. The real estate lady was there. She was kind; she had picked up some hamburgers and gave them to us. Soon we were driving up the mountain. It seemed as if we just came out of one turn when entering another turn. The engineer for that road must have been a swingy type.

After 27 miles of this kind of traveling we entered an unpaved logging road full of chuckholes and more turns. A song came to my mind, "Swing Me Home." After about ten miles, we arrived at the "promised land."

My heart sank as I looked at the long house, the roofing paper torn and waving in the wind. It was not much better on the inside. The place was cold. Buckets were placed here and there to catch the raindrops. Decon mouse poison boxes were placed in key positions for bait. The place was just used for vacations, and it looked forsaken. I just could not picture it as a home, no matter how hard I tried. It seemed as if all I could think of and see were negatives. No electricity, no phone—in fact, it is an unclaimed area as far as phone companies are concerned. I did not say much. My husband took a look at my disappointed face and said, "You don't like my Shangri-La?"

"No, I don't," was all I could whisper, tears dripping down my face.

We went outside to look around the property. There were three buildings, beside the house. One was a one-room house, listed as a guest house. The other was a work shop with three garages connected to it. The last building could be used as a barn with some work done on it. The land itself was a correction strip, 330 feet wide and about a mile long. Some pine trees, cedars, oaks and a great many rocks occupied the land. A year-round creek plowed through the property.

On the way down the mountain it was rather quiet in the car. I guess the real estate lady realized it was no use to try a sales talk.

Soon we were airborne, flying home.

For the next few days no one mentioned Shangri-La. But I could feel how sad Hans and the children were. They all liked the place so much. For them it had a challenge, so unexplored, so wild, a place to fish and hunt; one of the last frontiers on the continental U.S.A.

As the days went by, I began to search my heart. Was I standing against the will of the Lord for my family? We had prayed for a place. Was this the answer to our prayers? "Oh, Lord," was all I could say, "You know I just don't like that place, but if it is Your will for our family to move there, please help me to like it. Lord, I cannot see very far at all, I am so earth-bound, Your will be done, not mine."

I cannot say a miracle happened right away. But little by little I began to see some good points. Soon it was like a balanced scale, with negatives and positives even. Then the positives got heavier and heavier until I really found myself meditating upon the place a great deal without feeling hostile toward it. All this time I never let my family know what was happening. We just did not talk about the place any more.

One night we went to a meeting. The speaker was talking about the shape America is in. "Politically and financially, we are broke," he said. "It would be a blessing for Christians to provide for their families, and not depend so much on the system—have a garden, some animals and food stored up for the crises ahead. The cities will just be a death trap," he continued. "It would be better to live in a smaller town. The best of all is to live in the mountains someplace."

It was just as if he was talking to me. I knew what he said was true. My mind went back to my childhood, the terrible years of suffering. We had to depend upon God and hard work to survive. And I believe we survived because we were prepared. People got used to surviving, and knew how to fetch for themselves. Very little was available at the store. In the olden days they stored the food in their homes, but now it is only consumed there. How vulnerable we are now. I also remembered my fancy home in Edmonds. It was an all-electric house. One October we had a terrible storm that left us without power. How useless the place became. It was cold and dark, and in no way could we have a warm meal.

As we drove home, I said to my husband, "Honey, do you think the place we looked at is still available?"

"Perhaps, but I doubt it," he said, "it is three weeks since we looked at it. That place was quite unique. It could be sold."

"Please try to call them in the morning right early," I said.

"Are you sure you want it now?"

So I told him about my struggle, my prayers and how the Lord had been talking to me. "I appreciate that you did not press or talk me into moving, but that the Lord did the work."

Early the next morning we called the office. "Yes," they said, "we still have the place."

"Mark it sold," my husband said. "We are sending the down payment right away."

Later, the real estate lady told us that they had 73 requests for the place after we had bought it. It was just as if the Lord kept it for us until I could make up my mind.

Our Move Begins

Two months later we moved to Shangri-La. My circle had been completed. I was again among my friends—the woodstoves, kerosene lamps and scrub board. I had to think of a story a Canadian motel operator told us a few years back as we traveled in Canada. Another day had come to an end, and we rented a cabin. He then showed us how to operate the wood stove. "I grew up with one of them, so I know," I said.

"Good," he replied, "but you'd be surprised how many do not! A few days ago a young honeymoon couple from California rented this cabin. When I showed the bride how to use the stove, she clapped her hands in excitement and said, 'What will they think of next!'"

For me it was easy to adjust, for I had no romantic idea that moving to the mountain was going to be a life of ease. Some people think that moving into the woods is to sit under a tree, play the guitar and daydream.

Organic Gardening

Now it was April and time to start the garden. We had to begin from scratch. We decided to move our compost pile from Salem. It was a round trip of 540 miles, but we felt it was worth it. Compost is black gold. So with soil that we were able to scrape from among the rocks, the compost and some wood ashes, we started our garden. With great enthusiasm we planted the little seeds. After a couple of nice thundershowers we soon saw tiny plants peeking through the dark soil, and they really took off. The first we harvested were greens, onions and radishes. From then on we were in a land of plenty. What a surprise, what good eating, what a satisfaction and joy to pick from our own garden! We surely could notice a difference in our grocery bill, and also in the health and well-being of our family.

Animal Friends

The next step was to get the goats and the chickens. We had not moved everything from Salem. The house up there had not sold yet. So my husband brought a truckload every time he came. One night when he arrived, he kissed me hello, and asked if I had some milk for him.

"Not a drop in the house," I answered.

"Come and see," he said laughingly as he walked to the truck. "I brought you some fresh milk." The truck was bulging with animals. It reminded me of Noah's ark. Out came two milk goats, two young goats, three baby goats, two puppy dogs, two bantam hens with yellow chicks, and a mommy cat. The children were beside themselves with joy. They had living friends, not just some stuffed toys. The goats had to put on a dance right away. I am sure they were glad to get out of the truck. The area we live in is really a goat's paradise, rocks to dance and jump over. I watched baby goats play King of the Hill for the longest time. One would climb a rock, and others tried to take his place. They had a tug of war, and the strongest one won.

Goats have individual personalities. They know what they like and dislike. All our goats arrived with fancy names, but we renamed them. One we called "Nosy." She always peeked on, never missing a thing. One goat had a bell and she acted somewhat dumb. She was named Dumbbell. One had an even dark brown fur, so she became Brownie. And then we should not forget Trampoline; she liked to climb trees and people. She was forever stepping on us, or trying to put her hooves on our shoulders, while she looked straight into our eyes, as if to say, "Well, there you are, how about some grain?"

Goats browse like deer. Ours had small brush and scrub oak to feast upon. Later we bought two more milk goats. Now we had plenty of milk, not only for drinking, but also to make butter, yogurt and cottage cheese. I was able to buy a hand separator; a really nice floor model. I saved up milk until I had 10 gallons. To keep the milk fresh we put it into a gallon glass jar with a tight-fitting lid. The jars would be put into a wood-box and kept in the river. The box then was covered with two wet burlap sacks.

Our river is spring-fed and keeps an even temperature, summer and winter, of 47°F. The goat butter is white in color, quite different from store butter. But the taste is far superior. Now we had all the butter we needed. When we did not need the milk for butter, I made cottage cheese and yogurt. Cottage cheese was a good meat substitute. It tastes great when creamed, topped with chives and parsley and accompanied by new potatoes and a tossed salad.

Our dream was also to have some chickens; healthy ones, able to run free, and lay fertile eggs, with orange yolks. We bought 40 baby chicks from the hatchery. Twenty turned out to be roosters, and we had feasts on eighteen of them. They made good dinners, so different from the force-fed creatures with the watery taste that you buy in the supermarket. The hens more than supplied our egg requirements. We also sold a few and gave some away.

The first spring and summer at Shangri-La went so fast. The weather was perfect. There were warm sunny days and a blue sky, with only a couple of thundershowers, just enough to take the fire danger away and water the garden. If we got too hot, we just dove into the creek to cool off in a hurry. It was a happy time, although we had to work very hard. We fixed up the barn for the goats, and built a chicken-coop. Also, we roofed all the buildings.

Jesus Is In On The Final Move

Finally, in August our house was sold in Salem. A big moving van brought our belongings down. I decided to take a picture of the move. When the picture came back, I was so surprised to see not only the van and house in the picture but Jesus walking to the house. What had happened was that Tommy had decided to help the movers. He had gone into the van and taken a big picture of Jesus, held it on his back and walked to the house. It was strange that I did not notice this when I took the picture. Later on as I thought about it, my heart was warmed. How wonderful of Jesus to arrange this picture. I believe the message was for me. I was the one who did not like the place at first, but since I was willing to let Him decide what was best for us, He wanted to let me know He moved with us. Remember, when Peter had denied Jesus? Later, when Jesus was risen, He sent greetings to His disciples and a special greeting for Peter. Yes, Jesus can comfort. He is very tender and He knows our every need.

Our First Winter In The Mountains

Too soon the summer sun faded away. The nights got colder. The leaves turned yellow, brown, and reddish gold. Then they fell like telegrams from heaven. The message: Summer is over.

Now was the time to get our winter wood in, and do the hunting. We never cut live trees. There was plenty of dead wood just lying on the ground. Some of the trees had fallen from storms, others from old age. It takes so many years for a tree to mature; why waste a living tree? The whole family joined. Hans chain sawed; Roy, Tom and I took the bigger pieces and put them on the truck. Helen, Josef and Rose carried the smaller wood. What a joy it was to work together in the crisp autumn air. Soon rosy cheeks appeared, and at mealtime the food just disappeared. We were all so pleased when the last load went home. It was just in time, as dark clouds wrapped themselves around the mountain. Jack Frost nipped the air. Soon big white snowflakes came tumbling down.

My mind went back to the time when America was young and the first pioneers trailed westward. In spirit I was one of them. No wonder they celebrated Thanksgiving. It must have been a time of rejoicing when the harvest was in, and they could face the winter without fear. My heart was also filled with thanksgiving to the good Lord as I walked home. I could almost smell the turkey and pumpkin pie in the air.

That year we shot the deer so close that we brought it home in the wheelbarrow.

As fall progressed into winter, the days shortened. The sun kissed the mountains goodnight at four. The darkness came as a soft velvet cloth and draped the mountains in blues and purples. As I lit the kerosene lamp, my mind wandered back to my childhood days when I went with daddy to the lighthouse. I remembered how lovingly he tended to the light. What an important role the lighthouses played in guiding the ships safely into the harbor. As I looked upon my lamp, I wondered how my spiritual lamp was burning in the sight of God. Did I have enough oil; was my wick crusted over? How about the chimney—was it covered with smoke? "Oh, Lord," I whispered, "help my lamp to burn brightly." I love this song: "Let The Lower Lights Be Burning"!

1.　　Brightly beams our Father's mercy,
　　　From His lighthouse evermore,
　　　But to us He gives the keeping
　　　Of the lights along the shore.

2.　　Dark the nights of sin has settled,
　　　Loud the angry billows roar;

Eager eyes are watching, longing,
For the lights along the shore.

3. Trim your feeble lamp, my brother:
Some poor sailor tempest-tossed,
Trying now to make the harbor,
In the darkness may be lost.

Chorus: Let the lower lights be burning!
Send a gleam across the wave!
Some poor fainting, struggling seaman
You may rescue, you may save.

Evening time at Shangri-La would be our cozy time. The fireplace gave heat, and entertainment, too. Have you ever watched a snarled tree root burning? We cracked sunflower seeds from our garden, and talked as a family, perhaps sharing the happenings of the day. We read the Bible together and prayed. Our home was a real home, and God's peace was upon us. There was no T.V. blasting away, no brainwashing from commercials, no telephone to ring and disturb the peace. A good tiredness came over us, and we were so happy to have a bed.

The first winter in the mountains held some surprises for us. The house had only been used for a summer home and was extremely cold. Our water line froze, and now we had to carry water. Our wood disappeared rather quickly as we had to keep fires at night, when it was the coldest. We took the sled and went wood hunting in the winter wonderland. What a beauty our eyes beheld, snow-covered trees, and glistening white all around. No wonder the Bible says: ". . .*wash me, and I shall be whiter than snow*" (Psalm 51:7). The little children had a ride out, and the wood a ride home.

One of the goats Hans brought us had by now grown into a strong billy goat with a respectable beard. The children were sure he would be able to pull the sled. We made a harness for him, but he was a smart cookie. The only way we could get him to pull was when someone ran before him with a grain bucket.

We learned many valuable lessons in country living. Although our children couldn't go to school, that did not mean that they did not study. Grade school was 13½ miles away, and high school 37 miles, and there were no busses to pick them up. It would take about three hours a day hauling them ourselves. So we decided to teach them at home. We had some old school books. Hans was very good in math and English. We had spelling tests and math quizzes right around the kitchen table. I taught them carding, spinning, knitting and breadmaking. We realized that our school system was good, but not perfect. We needed to come up with a better program for the next winter.

The days got longer again, and the first signs of spring were the arrivals of our baby goats. What a happy occasion! Helen and Tom rejoiced as they rubbed the little creatures dry. Baby goats are so cute, so full of life and happiness, that one can't be sad for a minute if one watches them. Another winter storm came, and the children insisted that it was too cold for the newborns to be in the barn. So we brought a big box into the kitchen, lined it with hay, and set up our new nursery. Sometimes in the evening we took them out of the box and played with them. They were very clean, and seldom did they have an accident. But the joy they gave us made it worth while. Within three weeks we were blessed with ten of them. Luckily the weather turned warm and sunny and out they went. We bottle-fed them three times a day, which meant 30 bottles a day. A great deal of work, but what a "fun" time for the children.

We move to Shangri-La. Back row from left to right, Roy, Hans and Inger, Tom. Front row, young Josef, little Rose, and Helen.

"The first signs of spring were the arrivals of baby goats . . . Helen and Tom rejoiced as they rubbed the little creatures dry." Josef and Rose helped with the bottle-feeding three times day, which meant thirty bottles a day.

14

Sermons on the Mountain

"*And seeing the multitudes, he went up into a mountain: and when he was set, his disciples came unto him: And he opened his mouth, and taught them, saying,*" (Matthew 5:1-2). Yes, Jesus still teaches us in the solitude of the mountains.

I have often been asked this question: "Inger, are you not lonely when your husband and Roy leave on a speaking trip?" To be honest, there have been times when I felt lonely, and longing for fellowship. But the lessons I have learned from the nearness of Him who said, "*. . .I will never leave thee, nor forsake thee,*" (Heb. 13:5), have been engraved in my memory. One morning when I was feeding the chickens I noticed a hen had just hatched a bunch of baby chickens. Suddenly a hawk flew over, and instantly she spread her wings and covered her chicks. Then I remembered the Scripture: "*. . .how often would I have gathered thy children together, even as a hen gathered her chickens under her wings, and ye would not!*" (Matt. 23:37).

At times I also took the animals out to pasture. The sheep followed along nicely, but the goats fussed, taking a bite here and there. They had made up their minds about another route. They did not want to follow like the sheep. Again I was reminded of the Holy Scriptures where Jesus said that he would divide the sheep from the goats. "Lord, help me to have the nature of a sheep and not be as stubborn as the goats."

The Billy Goat And The Three Rainbows

I love rainbows. I feel they are a token of God's faithfulness, not only to Noah, but also to us. Many times I have been in need of an answer and then God would set a bow into the sky, and my faith took new courage.

One day we decided we had too many goats. So we moved the front seat out of Tommy's fastback Volkswagen and put in the big billy goat, three baby goats plus Tom, Josef, Rose and me. Needless to say, the car was full. The billy was put on the floor. We held one baby goat each; Tom, of course, was driving. The smell from the billy goat got really powerful in the car, but the trip to town went quite smoothly.

Since we lived so far from town, we always tried to combine many errands. I am not so sure my combination was too good that day. It was Thursday, animal auction day, and dentist appointment. We brought ropes along and tied down the goats in the backyard of the dentist's building. While the children had their teeth worked on, I was watching the rascals in the backyard. If the dentist had been the fussy type, the children could have returned right away with the Crest toothpaste commercial: "Look, mom, no cavities." But, as always, he gave us excellent service. He knew that if the work was not done today, it meant another 100-mile round trip for us.

We loaded the goats in the car again. This time, the billy was not too happy about riding. Too cramped in there, he muttered in his beard. "It should not be long now," we comforted him, "and you will soon have a new home. You know the grass is always greener on the other side." He seemed to relax a little and we drove on. When we came to the auction and checked in the animals, the first thing they asked as they looked upon billy was:

"Has he been de-scented?"

"Well, I am not sure what you mean," I said. "Helen scrubbed him with soap and water last night and he smells better today."

"No, no," they laughed. "Has he been to the veterinarian and had his scent glands removed?" The answer was no. "Then we cannot take him," they said. It was not a bit funny anymore —my heart just sank. Now we had to struggle with him again all the way home. And so we returned. On the road home the car was acting up. It did not seem to have any power. I looked back and said to Tom, "It is smoking a lot."

"Yes, it is overheated," he answered. So we stopped, let it cool off for a while, filled it with more oil and continued. As we started up the mountain, the car barely rolled. By now the billy was getting furious. His head was moving back and forth in a mad tempo. I was so sure he would knock the automatic transmission stick into reverse any moment. The next thing I expected was that he might jump through the front window. I started to sing to build up my faith.

"Got any rivers you think are uncrossable?
Got any mountains you can't tunnel through?
God specializes in things that are impossible
And He can do what no one else can do."

The answer came to me. *"Some trust in chariots, and some in horses: but we will remember the name of the Lord our God."* (Psalm 20:7) "Dear Lord, if we make it home, it's going to be a miracle. You see, our faith is so small; help us, dear Lord, amen." As I opened my eyes, I could not believe what I saw: three rainbows against the mountain; not one, but three. I knew then, we would make it home. My faith soared as I watched the beautiful sight. I am sure Noah himself could not have had any prettier display of rainbows. "Thank You, Lord, Oh thank You!" My eyes were filled with tears as I watched the glorious colors.

The car just kept rolling along slowly, but it was not stuttering so much. We reached the summit and it went faster downhill. I don't know who was the happiest when we reached home, the billy goat or we. He jumped out of the car faster than the lightning and ran over to the nanny goats. And there he complained long and hard to let them know how mistreated he was. As I closed my eyes that night, my heart was truly filled with thanks.

Superwoman

I cannot recall to this day what it was that my husband and I disagreed on. The main thing is that we had an argument. We were both disgusted. Then he said to me, "I want you to read Proverbs 31 to see how a real woman should behave."

I was still awfully mad when I started reading. I could see that I had measured up to many of the verses, but in many I had failed, too. When I came to verse 18 where it said: "*. . . her candle goeth not out by night,*" I closed the book and felt sorry for myself. Why had God made her into a superwoman? Her candle goeth not out by night! "You know, dear God, how tired I am when night cometh. I am more than happy to blow out my light. Against this woman I could not measure up. She was a superwoman beyond reach." When we are down in the dumps, that is when the enemy comes. He took me along, down Memory Lane, and I found myself sitting in rags with an empty stomach on a snow bank, watching the German soldiers march by in their warm wool uniforms and nice leather boots. They were singing "Deutschland, Deutschland über alles, über alles in der welt," which means "Germany, Germany, above all, above all in the world." It is the same spirit today, I thought, as I looked upon my German husband. I really felt sorry for myself.

But, you know, a family that prays together stays together. It did not take long at all before we were friends again. There are no perfect marriages. We must continually pray that the Lord blesses our union, and helps us to grow closer to Him, and closer to one another.

For many years I did not read about the Superwoman. Somehow I did not feel she was within reach. It was no use getting discouraged over her performance.

Then one day when I was doing the breakfast dishes and looking out the window, I saw the children taking the animals out to pasture. Our flock by now consisted of several milk goats with their baby goats, two Holstein calves, sheep, a donkey, not to forget our billy goat, who was still with us. I had to smile, as I watched the happy gang. My, how they all were growing big. Both the children and animals were really thriving. Within spoke the Lord: "Inger, remember the Scripture: *Her candle goeth not out by night?*"

"Yes, Lord, I remember; how could I forget?"

"When you blow out your lamp, you have things working for you, too. Look, the children, the animals, and the garden are all growing. The new honeybees are developing. The hens sitting on the eggs are faithfully at it even in the dark. Also, the yogurt you make in the evening is ready in the morning. Don't forget your sourdough and compost pile. You have much going for you, too."

My, it was like a revelation. I never thought of it that way. "Thank You, Lord, and forgive me for thinking that You were unjust in putting up her image." I left the dishes, took my Bible and read about my newly-found friend. Now I was rejoicing as I read about her, because I realized I could learn much from her. I may never be exactly like her; not even two snowflakes are alike. I have done things she never dreamed of, like logging 350 hours in a small airplane with my husband and children. I underlined verse 27: *"She looketh well to the ways of her household, and eateth not the bread of idleness."* My spirit was lifted up, as I put the Book away. How tender-hearted my heavenly Father was. "Thank You for the sermon, Lord."

The Generator Lesson

As time progressed, we bought a generator, which we installed in the work shop. Lines were laid to the house which was already wired. For many years they had a waterwheel that produced enough power for light and TV. This old waterwheel had been damaged by a flood one winter. It was beyond repair, and now only served as a landmark from the past. We hope one day when we have more time to build a turbine that can supply us with power. But for now I am happy about the generator. We can run it whenever we want. And when our work is finished, we turn it off. Our generator does not have much power, so I have learned to adjust. I know which appliances work together so I will not have an overload.

Once I started the generator, came back up to the house, and was going to vacuum clean. Nothing happened; the cleaner would not work. I made sure it was plugged in and the switch on. Could the vacuum cleaner be broken? I tried the blender: nothing happened. Something was fishy. I ran back to the work shop to see if the generator was running. I found it faithfully working. My eyes caught the problem. Above the motor is a switch. We can run the power for the work shop only, or switch it over to the house. I realized that the house was not connected to the generator. No wonder nothing worked! I quickly turned the switch on and ran back to the house. Now my appliances worked properly, for they had power. As I vacuum-cleaned it came to me how we as Christians are just like the appliances: we are able to produce only as we are tuned in to God. Christ said in John 15:5: *"I am the vine, ye are the branches: He that abideth in me, and I in him, the same bringeth forth much fruit: for without me ye can do nothing."* My generator is limited, but with God there is no limit. He is not poverty stricken, He is rich enough for all.

How important it is to seek Him in the morning. I like this poem, written by Ralph Cushman, called:

IN THE MORNING

I met God in the morning,
When my day was at its best
And His presence came like sunrise
Like a glory in my breast.
All day long the Presence lingered.
All day long He stayed with me.
And we sailed with perfect calmness
O'er a very troubled sea.
Other ships were blown and battered
Other ships were sore distressed.
But the winds that seemed to drive them
Brought to us a peace and rest.
Then I thought of other mornings
With a keen remorse of mind,

When I, too, had loosed the moorings
With the Presence left behind.
So I think I know the secret
Learned from many a troubled way.
You must seek God in the morning
If you want Him through the day.

God is not far off. He is real today. I often find myself talking to Him, or praising Him aloud. Perhaps I learned this from my mother. I can still remember how she talked to God. She was always very thankful, and found things to thank Him for, that most people take for granted. For example, she would say: "Thank You, Lord, for the sunshine; thank You, Lord, for the wind that dried my clothes." I believe the Lord is very pleased when His children are thankful. We read in the Bible about the times the children of Israel grumbled again, *and the Lord was sore displeased.* So, "Lord, help me to be thankful" is often my prayer.

The Bantam Hen And The Ducks

It is fun to watch nature and animals. I must tell you about our faithful little sitter. Perhaps many of you know that bantam hens just love to sit on eggs. You don't have to force them at all. They will gladly volunteer. We often used them as incubators for the Rhode Island Reds' eggs. We also let them sit on duck eggs. We had ducks, but they refused to sit in the chicken coop. They swam down or up the river and made their nests on an island, but wild animals consumed their eggs, and we never had ducklings. In the mornings Helen would keep them inside the chicken coop until they laid their eggs. When we had enough eggs, Helen placed them under the broody hen. We were all so excited: would the banty hen have enough patience? Chicken eggs take 21 days of sitting, but duck eggs 28 days. The calendar was marked for the great occasion. The bantam hen passed the test with flying colors. On the 29th day she came proudly marching out with five, fluffy ducklings. She paraded right before the rooster who lovingly looked at her little ones. I could almost hear him say,

"Well, Henny, Penny, no wonder I have not seen you for a long time. So, you have been sitting!"

"Yes," she said proudly, "how do you like my little ones?"

"Nice," he said, "but say, aren't the beaks and the feet a little different?"

Hurt, she looked at him and marched off. "Come, little ones, and let us have a dust bath. Nothing is wrong with you; how could that old rooster even mention such a thing?" She was a good little mother, and she diligently taught them all the tricks of the trade that good chickens should know. A few days of hard training seemed to bring them nowhere. She began to get a gnawing feeling that perhaps something *was* wrong. She decided to try a little longer; perhaps they were just a little slow, or perhaps on the lazy side. "Here I am, scratching my poor feet off, and they will gladly eat what I uncover, but I get no help to dig for the food."

Each day they wandered off a little farther from the chicken coop until one day they found the pond. What a happy day for the ducklings! They dove in as if they had been born in water. The poor hen just sat on the edge of the pond crying her heart out: her poor babies were drowning! As they became braver they ventured forth into the river. Now the poor hen was in real trouble. Running back and forth along the shore line, she clucked in a heart-rending way. When the ducklings reached the other side of the river, she flew across to rescue them.

Soon thereafter she left them for good; it was more than *she* could take.

The ducklings joined the other ducks and they explored the river. Now they were in their right place.

Beauty Versus Faithfulness

The drake we had was not very pretty. In fact, he was rather on the ugly side. He had lost one eye before he came to us, and that did not help his appearance at all.

We had some friends who also had ducks and they had a beautiful mallard drake that they wanted to give us. The next trip to town I picked him up and took him home in a cardboard box. As soon as he got among the ducks, he showed off. The other ducks walked down to the river, but not him, he flew. While out of sight he began to pick on the other drake to show him who was the big man on the river.

Soon the old drake got so sad; he had lost his kingdom. I think he died of a broken heart. Things changed in the duck family. Instead of coming home at choretime and spending the night safe and sound in the chicken coop, they stayed away. We now had to go down or up river to look for them. After a while it became a chore to bring them home. If we left them out, they would lose their lives to wild predators. So we killed them all. This is life. We have a saying in Norway that goes like this: "Not all things that glitter are gold."

15

Pioneering Together

Child Energy Channelled Into Fulfillment

Nowadays you hear so much about energy—how to save energy, how to harness energy. But in many homes across this great land, child energy is wasted. I love my children very dearly, and I think the best way to prepare them for the future is to teach them about the Lord and work. The Bible says in Prov. 22:6: *"Train up a child in the way he should go; and when he is old, he will not depart from it."*

When you work with children, you have to have a board meeting once in a while. Let them feel that you consider them very important, that you need their help, and that you are counting on them to get the work done. Children understand much more than we give them credit for. They love surprises, and, therefore, make the project a surprise for someone.

Once, when my husband and Roy were on a speaking trip, we wanted to have a surprise for them when they came home. We decided to paint the house. For a few months I had been picking up paint on special sales. We needed latex outdoor paint. Whenever I saw a really good buy, I bought a couple of cans. Most paint stores have a corner where they sell paint quite cheaply. At times they consist of colors that they had mixed for people but goofed on. To get rid of them, the stores let these paint cans go for a song. Finally, we had 12 gallons of different shades. No one could wait until all colors were mixed together to learn the final results. A big container was needed to hold all the gallons. We found an empty garbage can that we washed well and checked for leaks. Then we dumped all the paint into it, grabbed a big stick and started stirring. We had a joy dance when we saw the result. We wondered what to call our mix, and decided it was a HIT color, H for Helen, I for Inger, and T for Tommy. To explain the color to you, we called it Harvest Gold, but to us it was a HIT color.

Then all the old paint was scraped off. Next, we washed the whole house outside. Now we had to fill in the cracks and do the priming. It is very important to match the primer to the color that you are going to use, because this way the paint will cover the house better. With all the dirty work out of the way, we could now start the fun. Most children are fond of coloring; now they could color for real. A good time to start was early in the morning before it got too hot. Then, during the heat of the day, we took a break. Then was storytime, or we jumped on the bicycles and went to the swimming hole.

We were refreshed after the break, and happy to paint again. In the evening we judged our day's work and rejoiced as the house was taking on a new appearance before our very eyes. The drab colors disappeared as it was now having a face lift.

We finished in plenty of time before Hans and Roy returned. They were so happy when they saw what we had done and gave us a great deal of praise, which made up for all the hard work.

You cannot always have fun working. Sometimes the work is drab and dull. Then you must find something for encouragement to talk about, something to look forward to, like a fishing trip or a skiing trip. And when you promise, you must see to it that you do it. Perhaps I am just a kid at heart; that is why I enjoy working and playing with the children.

There are many other tasks that children can very easily do, like making beds, washing dishes, sweeping floors, chopping wood, feeding animals, cleaning chicken coops and barns, weeding, picking berries, helping with canning and making meals. We could go on and on. But there must also be a time for play and fun. There must be a balance. The good Lord will provide the balance as you ask Him for help.

If I were a working mother, I would not have the time and energy to work with my children. I would come home with a paycheck, but by the time I paid for a baby-sitter, hairdresser, new clothing, the second car, gas, repair and insurance, I am sure there would be little left, if any. Also, I would have to buy more ready-made food and clothing and make do with less help from the children because I could not be there to supervise them. Someone else would have to influence them. A baby-sitter does only what she is paid for. But by being with my children I can have a good influence. They are mine to mold, through my positive teaching and example. God entrusted them to my care. And by His grace I pray that I have not failed. When I leave this world, my hands are going to be empty—only the children, and the souls I won for Christ, will meet me on the other side. The Lord has given me the promise found in Isaiah 54:13: *"And all thy children shall be taught of the Lord; and great shall be the peace of thy children."* I am so thankful for this promise. Let me tell you it is not always fun to be around children and teach them. Sometimes it can be hard on the nerves.

As my girlfriend said, "I prayed for patience and God gave me a slow husband, and three kids that spill milk."

One time Josef was vacuum cleaning. He was doing really well and I was glad. But a few days later when I opened the vacuum cleaner I had a surprise. The bag that held the dust had disintegrated. The inside was rusted, and what a job it was to clean it. So I asked if he had vacuum cleaned water. "Yes," he answered, "some water was under the stove and it was sucked up." So he learned the lesson that one never puts water into a paper bag.

We inserted a new bag, and he was cleaning again in the hallway. Later I cleaned the living-room. I thought the vacuum cleaner sounded funny. So I opened it and found that the new bag was filled with burned holes. Josef was called on the scene and asked, "How come it is partly burned up?" He told me that he had vacuumed the spark guard in front of the stove. This time he learned the lesson never to vacuum-clean ashes unless he knew *for sure* they are dead. Sometimes they just look as if they are dead, but when they are sucked into the bag, they come alive. Josef looked at me and said, "Mom, I don't like vacuum cleaning. Those bags are so touchy and cannot take anything."

"Well, you are right, they *are* touchy, but now we have learned our lessons. We know what to look out for. Come to think of it, the lessons we just learned remind me of the earth's history. We read in the Bible that the earth became so wicked and sinful that God destroyed it by water. In Peter we read that next time He will cleanse it by fire." He smiled and understood. We put our last bag in and continued our cleaning.

Perhaps cleaning is not his strongest point, but when it comes to wood chopping, he is tremendous. He handles the axe with power and accuracy. My wood box is always filled, although he sometimes teases me and says that I must have a hole in the box because the wood disappears so fast.

We seldom pay the children for helping us. Hans and I grew up helping our parents and never got paid. Any money we needed had to be earned outside the home. So I used my spare time baiting fish hooks for the fishermen. Sometimes I could bait over 2000 hooks in one day. It was cold, hard work, but I had the joy of earning my own money. So when we moved out to the country I wondered how the children could make money. Since we had no close neighbor, they could not baby-sit or cut the lawn. Through my battle against cancer I had learned about herbs and what grows in our area. Now we took our baskets and went out to gather herbs. We learned when to pick and how to dry and prepare them properly for the market. It is a joy to take the basket and walk through forests, meadows and along creek sides. Many treasures are found while the birds sing for us. It is such a good feeling to know what you pick is organic and unpolluted. The place is so untouched by man, only God providing the rain and sunshine.

Herbs should dry in the shade. Therefore, I put a clothesline between two oak trees that provided shade all day long. In the material store I bought nylon netting by the yards. I put the herbs loosely into the netting, and fastened it to the line with clothespins. Once in a while I rearranged the herbs so that the inside will also dry. When absolutely dry, I dumped the bag on my kitchen table and we sorted through it, removing stems and branches. Then there is the joyful moment when we can sell it. We also sell fresh watercress in the springtime and fall. We bundle it up, put a rubber band around each bundle, and off to market it goes. In the summer months the watercress blooms and is too hot to eat. We never had any trouble selling our products.

Some years the trees are loaded with cones, and timber companies will buy cones by the bushels. It is enjoyable work, and well paid, but we have to climb trees and knock the cones down with an old broom handle. Sometimes we pick high in the treetops, and should our feet slip, it would be a long fall, and below, the ground is studded with rocks. We could easily get hurt. I am always so happy when the cone season is over.

We have learned a lot from different projects, and also had some profit. Sometimes we divide the money and each child gets his share; other times we save for something very special, for instance, when my husband and Roy spoke again in the Los Angeles area. The rest of the family could go to visit them and also see Disneyland and Knott's Berry Farm from the money made off herbs and watercress. At times I wonder what was more fun, working, talking and dreaming about it, or actually doing the thing we saved for? Thus, the Lord always provides for our every need.

Spicing Up Life

Aside from the money aspect, I have really fallen in love with herbs. They add so much to one's life. In my garden I reserved a small area for growing them. There you will find parsley, chives, dill, horse radish, winter savory, English thyme, sage, tarragon, oregano, sweet basil, lemon balm and orange mint. In the creek nearby grows an abundance of spearmint and peppermint. The precious herbs add so much flavor to our meals. In the summertime we can use them fresh from the garden. In the winter, of course, we use them dried. They take very little care, and give such a gift of flavors all year long. I have made a tea mixture of different herbs, and when served for guests, I always get a great many compliments. It is good to the last drop.

If you don't know anything about herbs, you are in the same shoes I was in when I moved to the mountains. But you can learn so much by borrowing books from the library on the subject, and also by asking anyone in your area who has a knowledge about herbs. Some people think that a cup of tea is going to cure them of all ills. I believe it takes more than that. Happiness and health is to know the Savior first of all. Then, to get much fresh air and exercise and to use fresh organic food eaten raw as much as possible. You can add herbs to flavor your life.

Stalking The Wild

Stalking the wild for salad greens has been a great help, especially in the early spring before we can eat from the garden. The young dandelion shoots and buds can be eaten; later some marshmallow, lamb's quarter, purselane, and chickweed. They are loaded with vitamins and minerals. While watery lettuce is selling at the grocery store for $.79 a lb., I get my greens for nothing, plus a lot of sunshine, fresh air and exercise as a bonus. And as I am picking, I can talk to the Lord and praise Him for all things He has made.

I must tell you about Rosi and Josef and how they were living off the land. From the time they were small I always took them along when gathering our salad. I showed them what to pick, and told them to be extremely careful not to pick or eat anything else.

One day we were having lunch and they said they were not hungry. They must be sick, I thought, and felt their foreheads, but no, they did not feel warm. The next meal was the same thing, not hungry. Now I was suspicious that something was going on. I knew for sure they had not been snacking, and nobody else could have given them food, because they had been just outside the house, playing. I knew they were in the fort they had built in the forest. I went up there ever so quietly and peeked through the logs, and there they sat on the floor like two Indians, eating wild greens they had picked themselves. I had to smile—so, that was the reason for not being hungry. They were living off the land, and only four and five years old. My husband sometimes helped me pick. He likes the dandelion buds a lot. One day he brought me a bowl of these buds only. "This is your snack," he said. I thanked him and started to eat. Then I got busy making bread and forgot about my snack. A couple of hours later I remembered my present and looked for my bowl. What a surprise! The buds had turned into flowers. Those bright-eyed yellow fellows smiled at me, and I could not help but smile back. Their transferral from the cold April morning into my cozy warm kitchen had made them unfold. If they did have stems, I could put them in a vase; but now, what could I do but eat them anyway?

Mushrooms are a delight. You have to be doubly sure you know what you pick. Mushrooms can turn an ordinary meal into a gourmet dinner. Hans learned a lot about mushrooms during the five years his family spent in East Germany under Communism. He picked mushrooms for us. One kind looked just like another we had been eating. The only difference was that the flesh turned light blue when cut with a knife. One day I drove to town to do some shopping. I brought one of these mushrooms along to show a friend. He said, "They are poisonous, and you must not eat them."

In the evening, as I drove home, I met my sweet husband walking along the logging road. I stopped the car, kissed him, and began to talk. "What a peaceful evening," he said as his eyes looked lovingly at the countryside. The orange sun was just kissing the mountain range good-night. The last sunbeams made the pine trees glimmer. The oaks smelled sweet after a warm day. We stood there just holding hands and enjoying the sunset. Suddenly I asked, "Have you eaten dinner?"

"Yes, Tom and I ate half an hour ago."

"What did you eat?" I asked.

"A big panful of mushrooms, and did they ever taste good!"

"You did not eat those that turn blue when you cut them?"

"Yes," he said, "those were the ones we ate."

"But, honey, they are poison and you are in trouble. Petri's mushroom book said they should not be eaten!"

"I am sure they are all right—we used to eat them in Germany."

"But, honey, we are in America and the book said not to eat them. Jump in the car and let us go home and see what we can do." Suddenly the evening was not peaceful anymore. Time was running out! Hans and Tom had to do something. They put their fingers in their throats and threw up. Then they drank half a gallon of goat milk to dilute the poison. Both of them lived through the night. Hans said he felt a little giddy in his head, but not too bad. Finally, the rays of a new day began. Hans and Tom were alive and well. Perhaps the mushrooms were not poisonous after all? Or perhaps their time was not up yet?

Alternate Education

Perhaps by now you wonder how we came along with the children's education. Looking back on the eight years we lived in our mountains, I was pleased. The first year was rather hit and miss. We were teaching them, but did not have a program to follow. I will give you a rundown on each child.

Roy took 8th grade by correspondence through a private Christian school in California while he was on the nine-month speaking tour with his dad. The school work was done whenever there was a spare moment. That spare moment could be while waiting for someone to pick them up from the airport, or for the meeting to start. He did so well that I will never forget the letter we received from the principal:

BACK TO GOD IN EDUCATION
Escondido Christian School

COURSES OF STUDY FOR	POST OFFICE BOX 715
KINDERGARTEN	ESCONDIDO, CALIFORNIA 92025
THROUGH GRADE 8	TELEPHONE 745-2071

August 9, 1972

Dear Rev. and Mrs. Schneider,

This is to inform you that your son, Roy Sigvart Wathne, has successfully completed his 8th grade correspondence course at the Escondido Christian School. His grades are as follows:

Social Studies	A	Spelling	A
Science	B	Health	A
Math	A−	Geography	A

His work shows completeness, forethought, and maturity. The course of study is rigorous and demanding! It is with pride that we compliment you and your ministry's effect on your son's life. I hope that my new son, Kevin, only 4 weeks of age, learns about the Lord and his academic studies as readily.

If I can be of any other service to you, please notify us. The Lord continue to bless you and your ministry.

Yours in His service,

Rev. T. G. Paterson, Jr.
Principal

carbon copy to:
Walker Jr. High School

"Train up a child in the way he should go: and when he is old, he will not depart from it." Proverbs 22:6

Then Roy took high school through American School in Chicago. Most of the school work was done while traveling, or in the dead of winter when he was home. Roy finished high school with flying colors. He did so well that he received a scholarship of $400. Out of 90,000 students only 22 got this award. So it was a great honor to be among the few. The local newspaper honored him with the following article in September of 1977:

ASHLAND MAN AWARDED $400 SCHOLARSHIP

Roy Wathne-Schneider of Ashland has been awarded a $400 College Scholarship by American School, 850 E 58th St., Chicago, Illinois.

Each year a select number of American School graduates are awarded college scholarships ranging from several hundred dollars to $2,000. Students are selected on the basis of academic achievement, community activity, and personal integrity.

American School is reportedly the largest high school in the world providing high school education by correspondence. Founded in 1897, American School is a fully accredited non-profit educational institution.

Roy is the public relations agent and secretary for his father, Hans J. Schneider, author and evangelist lecturer.

Roy plans to use his scholarship to further his education at Southern Oregon State College, where he is currently an honor student. He hopes to go into the publishing business after college.

Next was college, and he stayed on the honor roll throughout college.

Tommy took 8th grade through correspondence. Then he, like Roy, enrolled with the American High School in Chicago. Tom did well, too, and in college he also stayed on the honor roll.

Helen took the 7th grade by correspondence. During eighth grade she went to a little mountain school about 13½ miles away. High school was taken through the Ashland Adult Learning Center. She did the assignments at home. Whenever I went shopping, I took her along and dropped her off at the Center. They corrected Helen's homework and helped her if she had any problems. New assignments were given and she could go home and do more schoolwork. When ready, she took the tests and passed, only 17 years old. At 18 she started college, where she is majoring in business administration.

Josef and **Rosi** started school at home when only four and five years old. Helen taught them kindergarten and first grade. Then they went to the mountain school through 4th grade. Last winter we borrowed books there and taught them at home. I am learning along with the children. My favorite subject is American history. There are plenty of heroes in my kitchen. As we read about the Declaration of Independence, we can visualize John Hancock, the first one to sign. He wrote big letters. "There," said he, "King George will have no trouble reading this, even without spectacles."

"Gentlemen, we must all hang together now," said Benjamin Franklin as he took up the quill, "or we will all hang separately." Unafraid, they signed. Also exciting is the Boston Tea Party. Next, we read about General Marion, who was known as the Swamp Fox. In 1780 a British officer came to him with a flag of truce. They talked together and Marion said: "I am in love and my sweetheart is liberty." The English officer reported later to his soldiers, "I saw an American general, and his soldiers without pay, almost without clothes, living on roots, yet they endure all the hardship for liberty. What chance do we have against such men?"

The history hour goes by too quickly. Next is recess, and that can be bottle-feeding the baby goats, trying the ice on the pond, or perhaps the new snow is just begging to be formed into a snowman.

For reading we choose different stories. May we share with you the story of the Little Red Hen. It brings us up-to-date, where we are as a country today. It is a sad but true picture.

LITTLE RED HEN

Once upon a time, there was a little red hen who scratched about and uncovered some grains of wheat. She called her barnyard neighbors and said, "If we work together and plant this wheat, we will have some fine bread to eat. Who will help me plant the wheat?"

"Not I," said the cow.

"Not I," said the duck.

"Not I," said the goose.

"Then I will," said the little red hen, and she did.

The wheat grew tall and ripened into golden grain. "Who will help me reap my wheat?" asked the little red hen.

"Not I," said the duck.

"Out of my classification," said the pig.

"I'd lose my seniority," said the cow.

"I'd lose my unemployment insurance," said the goose.

Then it came time to bake the bread.

"That's overtime for me," said the cow.

"I'm a dropout and never learned how," said the duck.

"I'd lose my welfare benefits," said the pig.

"If I'm the only one helping, that's discrimination," said the goose.

"Then I will," said the little red hen. And she did. She baked five loaves of fine bread and held them all up for the neighbors to see. They all wanted some, demanded a share. But the red hen said, "No. I can rest for a while and eat the five loaves myself."

"Excess profits," cried the cow.

"Capitalistic leech," screamed the duck.

"Company fink," grunted the pig.

"Equal rights," yelled the goose. And they hurriedly painted picket signs and marched around the little red hen singing, "We shall overcome," and they did.

For when the farmer came, he said, "You must not be greedy, little red hen. Look at the oppressed cow. Look at the disadvantaged duck. Look at the underprivileged pig. Look at the less fortunate goose. You are guilty of making second-class citizens of them."

"But . . . but," said the little red hen. "I earned the bread."

"Exactly," said the wise farmer. "That is the wonderful free enterprise system; anybody in the barnyard can earn as much as he wants. You should be happy to have this freedom. In other barnyards, you'd have to give all five loaves to the farmer. Here you give four loaves to your suffering neighbors." And they lived happily ever after, including the little red hen, who smiled and clucked: "I am grateful. I am grateful."

But her neighbors wondered why she never baked any more bread. END

—Compliments of Instant Printing Center

In our school there is no law against prayer or Bible study. We can pray any time we want and ask the good Lord for wisdom. We know God was very pleased when Solomon asked for wisdom. We also read that David behaved himself wisely. The Lord Jesus Christ grew in wisdom and knowledge. And let us not forget about James who writes: *"If any of you lack wisdom, let him ask of God, that giveth to all men liberally, and upbraideth not; and it shall be given him."* (James 1:5)

The busiest year we had was the year we tackled five different grades—kindergarten, first grade, seventh grade, eighth grade and high school. Someone was studying in every corner. I called it the year of brain expansion.

One of the major keys in successful learning is discipline. It is impossible to get ahead without it. Also, you must obey the rules of your state concerning the legality of educating your own children. We could do it lawfully because we lived so far from school.

Decorating On A Shoestring

There is much you can do to improve your house and make it more cheerful and cozy, without spending a fortune. Many urgent things had to be repaired and built outside before we could begin to think of the inside of the house. But finally the time came when I could see hope in sight.

We decided to have a garage sale in town to make money. So we loaded up the truck with odds and ends we did not need anymore. It was fun to meet so many friendly people. During the sale we gave out Bible tracts and Christian books to buyers and non-buyers. The sale gave us $100, enough to buy Formica for the kitchen. We chose a yellow, warm pattern. Brother Abbott, a friend of ours, and Tom installed it. What a difference it made, so easy to keep clean and also so cheerful. Gone were the rough wood boards with all the cracks in them. Next, we wanted to paint the kitchen ceiling and windows. I decided to wallpaper the walls. For a long time I had been picking up paint from garage sales and stores whenever the price was really low. The great day finally arrived. It is always so exciting to mix the paint together. I counted 14 different quart containers, none of the same color. I could hardly wait to see what shade we would get, mixing them all together. We started out slowly, pouring one can at a time, sitrring thoroughly. If there are lumps, the paint can be strained through an old nylon stocking.

I had an idea what color I wanted, so whenever a bargain came along, I had to be sure it would blend in with the rest. To our surprise, a lovely light cream beige came forth from the mixing, just the shade I had hoped for. All the paint did not come to more than $9. The ceiling was scrubbed down. We wanted to be sure that the surface we painted was clean. Any cracks had to be filled. Then came the fun part and that was to roll on the paint. The children enjoyed the project as much as I did. They all wanted to be right there to help. Tom seemed to have a knack for wall papering, painting, floor laying and repair, which came in handy.

The wallpaper we chose for the kitchen was an apple and pear pattern with green leaves, which added warmth to our country kitchen. We bought the paper on sale for fifty cents a roll.

At last came the floor. We went to a warehouse and sorted through boxes. They were having a sale and we could get tiles for ten cents each. The kitchen is big and we didn't find enough of one color to cover it. We chose two different colors that blended nicely and put them in a checkerboard pattern. The whole kitchen decorating came to about $200. It really made the room so much cozier, and the joy of doing it ourselves cannot be described. Great lessons for all of us! We were so pleased, that we decided to go through the whole house, taking one room at a time. Now we enjoy our home even more.

16

Spiritual Nuggets of Daily Living

As we walk with the Lord, we learn new lessons every day. Some we forget, but others are engraved into our memories and, no matter how many years pass by, we always recall them. I will share with you a few things that have been really precious to me.

The Prepared Chariot

Jesus has called us to be witnesses for Him, but often we see little result from our effort. My friend Ardis was different. Ever so often, a few of us gathered together for a time of sharing and prayer. Ardis usually gave the most glorious testimonies of leading someone to Christ. After listening and rejoicing with her, we began to realize that she was operating differently from us.

Finally, one day we asked her why she had success, while our witnessing was hit and miss, mostly miss. She then told us about Philip and how God told him to sit by the wayside and wait for that special chariot to come along *"Then the Spirit said unto Philip, Go near, and join thyself to this chariot"* (Acts 8:29). He went and asked the man if he understood what he was reading. The unuch replied: *" . . . How can I, except some man should guide me?"* (Acts 8:31). So Philip climbed into the chariot and preached Jesus unto him. The eunuch was saved, baptized and went his way rejoicing.

"I always was thriled by this story," Ardis continued. She went on, "I realized I could waste my time talking to people who were not prepared. I began asking the Lord to lead me to a prepared chariot, someone who was hungry for God, someone who was searching for true meaning in life." God had truly answered her prayer.

One day as Ardis was praying for her unsaved husband, the Lord seemed to say, "Ardis, you've asked me for such a long time to save him. Why don't you trust Me for his salvation? Instead of asking Me to save him, why don't you thank Me for saving him?" So Ardis did just that. She praised the Lord for saving him. Shortly after that, her husband was saved! God honored her faith.

The Blessing Of The Lord

" . . . *it maketh rich, and He addeth no sorrow with it"* (Prov. 10:22).

I like this verse, because I know it is so true. It is better to have the blessing of the Lord in your home, than all the riches this world can offer. The word blessing means divine favor. As I recall my childhood, I know for sure we had God's blessing upon our home. It was because Mother always asked the Lord to bless everything we had, and He did, and she always thanked Him for it.

Perhaps little Rose explained the blessing best. We had just milked the goats, gathered the eggs, and with the last ray of daylight we were picking strawberries in the garden. Soon the day faded away, and God lit His stars. We stood in the garden for a moment, just to smell the fragrance of the earth and growing things. She took my hand as we walked to the house and said: "Mom, truly the Lord has blessed us." She was only four years old when she said that, but I know that she fully understood God's blessing.

When God blesses something, there is always plenty to go around. Jesus blessed a little boy's lunch, and there was enough to feed the multitude. They even gathered up the fragments and had twelve baskets full. And here, I believe, Jesus taught us the secret of God's blessing is not to waste any food, but carefully to gather up all the crumbs. And this lesson applies to other things as well. We just don't throw away clothing or furniture because they are not in style. We use them anyhow and thank God for them.

"We stood in the garden for a moment, just to smell the fragrance of the earth and growing things. Rose took my hand as we walked to the house and said: 'Mom, truly the Lord has blessed us.'"

17

Sudden Death Strikes
My First-Born

Suspicious News And A Long Wait

It was the last day of March, 1980. I was doing the breakfast dishes. As I looked out the window, I saw a police car at the gate. My heart jumped. What message was he coming with? Had Hans, Roy, Helen, Josef and Rosi crashed as they were heading for town? I could feel my heart in my throat as I opened the door for him.

"Good morning," he said. "Are you Mrs. Schneider?"

"Yes, I am," was all I could utter.

"Does Roy live here?"

"Yes, he does, he is my oldest son."

"The doctor sent me to tell Roy that he must come to his office immediately."

"What is the matter?" I asked.

"I don't know too much," he answered, "but Roy's white blood count is too high."

"Roy left for college this morning. Could you be so kind when you get to town to contact my husband at our town address and tell him to get in touch with Roy and the doctor right away."

"I will be glad to do so," he answered kindly, and drove off.

As he left, I had to sit down for a moment to think. "It must be dangerous and it must be urgent since the doctor sent him all the way up here. But what could it be?"

At the end of the winter term in college I had noticed that Roy looked a little pale. He had a cold, a headache, and ran a fever for a few days. We thought he caught the flu that was going around. At this time Roy also needed his physical examination for his pilot's license. This would reveal any possible health problems. So, on Friday afternoon, the week before, we went to the doctor and Roy passed his exam.

"I cannot find anything wrong with him," the doctor said.

"Please make a blood test," I pleaded, and he did. Since the office was just about to close, I told him that Roy could contact him on Monday after his college classes for the result.

I could not work after the policeman left. I spent my time in Bible reading and prayer, but there seemed to be no comfort. Oh, how I wished I had a phone. I looked at the truck; should I take it and drive to town? Then I glanced at the snow-covered road and decided to stay home. I was not a very good driver in snow. The day went by ever so slowly.

Facing The Grim Facts

Finally, I could see the headlights of our car coming down the road. I threw a coat on and ran out to meet them. One look at my husband caused me to realize how grave the situation must be. We went inside, and my husband said, "I am afraid I have bad news for you. Roy has acute leukemia. The doctor wanted him in the hospital right away to start chemotherapy. But I have heard a lot of bad reports about chemotherapy. I want us to fly him down to a clinic in Mexico where they treat patients along natural lines, with fresh juices and live food."

"That will be best," I said. "Let us just get Roy to bed and start early in the morning." I took a look at Roy; he looked tired, but he was brave. He still ate the evening meal, and went to bed. My husband I went to the office and started to look for the address of the clinic. We wanted to get the best help for Roy; nothing would be too good for him. I decided to sleep in a bed next to Roy. If he needed any help, I would be right there.

A Night Of Agony

Sleep hardly came; my heart was just aching. "Oh, dear God, be merciful—please let him get well," was my prayer over and over. I must have spent a few minutes in the land of Nod, for I woke up and heard Roy saying, "This is the end." I ran over to his bed and said,

"What's the matter, honey?"

"This is the end," he said. I rushed to my husband, and told him what Roy had just said. We lit a lamp and went to his aid. He was now bleeding through his nose and had trouble breathing. *"The one way is the right way,"* he said, and then he became unconscious.

"We must get an ambulance quickly!" Hans demanded. "Do you want to stay here with Roy, and I drive for help, or do you want to drive?"

I knew my husband would keep calm and be better help for Roy. So I decided to drive. I jumped into the car around 3:00 A.M., not worrying about the snow, just driving the 13½ miles to a telephone booth. My hands were so cold I could hardly dial the number. I explained to the driver where he could find me. Next, I called the doctor. He promised to meet us at the emergency room at the hospital. Tom was going to Rogue Community College in Grants Pass, 70 miles farther north. He also needed to be informed. I called him and told him to meet us at the hospital.

I knew it would be more than one hour before the ambulance could arrive. It was snowing. The road was covered with ice and snow. Above it lay a thick layer of fog. Only the tops of the mountains peaked through the fog, and they were draped in a dark, foreboding veil. It was just as if nature was sorrowing with me. My feet began to feel numb from the cold. My heart was aching, and tears were streaming down my face. I began to walk back and forth on the road before the telephone booth to keep warm. "How could it be, Lord? Roy left for school just a few hours ago, and now he is dying! My precious boy, so young, too young to die. Oh Lord, if I only could see a rainbow." I remembered so many times before, when I had been in distress and the Lord put a bow into the sky to lift my faith, and encourage me. But there was no rainbow, only icy cold snowflakes that mingled with my tears.

Reflections About Roy

Like a flash through my mind I recalled the morning 22 years ago when Roy was born. What a day of pure heavenly joy! A lovely spring morning with cherry blossoms just unfolding . . . and then the sun disappeared and it started snowing. Big cold flakes covered the blossoms. And now Roy, just on the threshold of life, was facing the grim reaper who was trying to snatch his life away.

Roy's life seemed to pass like a movie before me. He was always a joy to be around. Once he came home from school after his own father had died and found me crying. "But, mom, don't cry—remember, underneath are the everlasting arms of God."

He was only 13 years old when he began to evangelize with his new dad. I told Roy, "If Dad wants you to speak, remember, you stutter when you try to explain something. Just learn a few Bible verses by heart and say them." As they left, I could not help but think of the Apostle Paul and young Timothy.

To my great surprise, not long after they were gone I received a tape, and on it Roy was preaching. I could not believe my own ears. His stuttering was all gone, and he preached a wonderful sermon. I knew the Lord had touched his lips. Soon letters came from people who had listened to him and were blessed. He was known as the little boy preacher. The trip lasted nine months. Many more journeys followed as they crisscrossed America, telling the good news.

Roy also liked gardening. Whatever spare time he had, he spent working in the garden. I still hear him say, "Mom, one day we will have a greenhouse." Because of our altitude we have late frost in the spring, and with a greenhouse we could get an early start.

A Quick Departure

The ambulance finally arrived and I jumped in. Two young men were in the car. "Sorry it took us such a long time, but the snow and fog slowed us down." I gave them a short report of Roy's condition.

I was hoping for some good news when we came back home, but Roy was still unconscious and had trouble breathing. He was quickly transferred into the ambulance and my husband and I rode along. When we arrived at the telephone booth, I picked up the car I left there, and drove behind the ambulance down the mountain.

When we entered the hospital emergency room, Tom was there. He was so shocked to learn that his brother was extremely ill. While the doctors and nurses took care of Roy, Hans, Tom and I went to the chapel to pray. But oh, how hard it was to pray. I felt that heaven was made out of solid brass. There was no answer, no hope, no relief.

The doctor came and talked to us. He said that they had done what they could for Roy, but he was not responding. The brain scan was negative. Roy was only kept alive through artificial breathing, and the heart machine. As soon as the decision had to be made to disconnect the machines, he would die. The doctor urged us to give our permission as soon as possible as there was no hope. What a hard decision to make, but since the brain was destroyed, we had no choice. As we returned to Roy's room, we could see his quiet, sheet-covered body on the bed. Tubes led to and from him like wires on a switchboard. We watched, heart broken, as the tubes were disconnected one by one. Soon the heart took its last beat.

The chaplain and the nurses treated us ever so kindly. "You must be used to this," I said to them.

"No," they answered. "We never get used to someone dying. Death is always hard to take, especially when someone is so young, and dies so quickly."

Never Without Comfort

As we came home, I took the Book of Comfort and asked the Lord for a verse to hang my sorrow on. And He gave me Isaiah 57:1—*"The righteous perisheth, and no man layeth it to heart; and merciful men are taken away, none considering that the righteous is taken away from the evil to come."* "Lord," I whispered, "You took Roy away from evil to come. You know what is best. Although my heart is aching, I must say with Job of old, *'Though He slay me, yet will I trust in Him'"* (Job 13:15).

I Will Not Doubt

I will not doubt, though all my ships at sea
    Come drifting home with broken masts and sails;
    I shall believe the Hand which never fails,
From seeming evil worketh good for me.
    And though I weep because those sails are tattered,
    Still will I cry, while my best hopes lie shattered:
      "I trust in Thee."

I grew up by the sea and listened to the fishermen talking. I still can hear one of them say: "In fierce storm we must do one thing and that is to put the ship in a certain position and keep it there until the storm is over." Sometimes we are like Paul—we can see neither sun nor stars, and no small tempest lies on us. Our reasoning does not help us. Our eyesight is far too dim. Then we must trust in God's everlasting faithfulness and love through Christ Jesus our Savior. Yes, tears will still flow, but there is a difference for the believer. A child of God sorrows with hope. What a comfort it is to read I Thessalonians 4:13-18: *"But I would not have you to be ignorant, brethren, concerning them which are asleep, that ye sorrow not, even as others which have no hope. For if we believe that Jesus died and rose again, even so them also which sleep in Jesus will God bring with him. For this we say unto you by the word of the Lord, that ye which are alive and remain unto the coming of the Lord shall not prevent them which are asleep. For the Lord himself shall descend from heaven with a shout, with the voice of the archangel, and with the trump of God: and the dead in Christ shall rise first: Then we which are alive and remain shall be caught up together with them in the clouds, to meet the Lord in the air: and so shall we ever be with the Lord. Wherefore comfort one another with these words."*

Many letters and cards of sympathy arrived. They were really heart warming. We live in such a busy world, but people still care and respond. I think that is wonderful. I would like to share one of the letters with you.

Southern Oregon State College
Business Division / 482–6484

April 3, 1980

Dear Mr. and Mrs. Hans Schneider:

We wish to express our deepest sorrow for your loss of Roy. He was "our" loss also. We both knew Roy very well and admired his extremely fine academic ability, mental sharpness, and willingness to work. It'll be a long time before the School of Business has another student with so much native business knowledge.

We both had numerous occasions to get to know Roy and we feel terribly shocked that someone so young could die so quickly. However, be assured, Mr. and Mrs. Schneider, that Roy accomplished more in his 22 short years than others do in 50 or 60 years. He worked so hard!!

Yes, we both believe the "good ones die young" and Roy was one of the best. He added so much to the classroom situation. Roy was never passive—*always* involved. He was always one you could count on to have the answer. Students learned so much from him.

We feel saddened that we will never have Roy in our midst again . . . Yet we know he's always here!

Sincerely,

Jerry A. Cooper
Associate Professor of Business

Tom Hitzelberger
Associate Professor of Business

18

A Trip to Europe
Was Like Medicine

Wherever we looked, something reminded us of Roy. When I went out into the garden, I looked at the young fruit trees just planted by Roy a few days before his departure. My husband could not stay in the office. Roy's empty desk, next to his, was more than he could take. I watched Hans's hair turn grey in a short time. "You know, Inger," he said, one day, "I lost more than a son, I lost a friend."

We needed to get away awhile. "How about going to the land of the midnight sun?" I said. "Hans, we have been married almost 13 years and you have never met my mother or brothers. You have traveled in almost 100 countries but never in Norway. And I have never been in Germany to visit your mother." So we decided to go and take Josef and Rose Sharon along. Tom and Helen stayed at home and took care of the garden, animals and the business for us. How we wished we all could go together, but it was impossible. We promised Tom and Helen that they could go when we came back.

On August 6th, 1980, a big Boeing 707 winged us from San Francisco, to Frankfurt, Germany. From there we took the train to Hans's mother and stepfather: so good for us to see them again, and for me and the children to discover Germany.

Beyond The Arctic Circle

There we bought a used car. We figured that would be the cheapest way of traveling. Mom Schneider lent us blankets, pillows and camping gear. Soon we were driving north, north, to the northernmost village on the European mainland. On the way we passed through part of Germany, all of Denmark, and part of Sweden. There we took the ferry from Stockholm to Turku, Finland, which took a whole day. We really enjoyed the lovely scenery. On the ship they served the biggest smörgåsbord I ever saw, the best food I ever tasted. Then we continued through Finland, the land of the 1000 lakes. The trees got smaller and smaller until they finally disappeared completely. Also, the air became cooler as we journeyed northward. Soon the day arrived when we crossed the border into Norway.

So good to hear my native language again and see the friendly smiles, the blue, blue ocean, and the blue, blue eyes. Our first stop was with my brother Ottar who lives close to Russia. The next day we drove along the Russian border. We saw the barbed-wire fences and the manned watchtowers. One was not even allowed to take a picture toward Russia. It looked like a prison camp. Our eyes gazed across the barbed-wire fence. On one side was freedom and happiness, on the other a godless nation in slavery.

Now we were on our last leg. A few more hours of driving and we would arrive in Gamvik, my birthplace. It was so good to see dear Mom and my oldest brother Rolf again. And they rejoiced also to meet Hans, Josef and Rose, whom they had never met before. Hans and the children really enjoyed the stay, although the language was a problem; but a smile and a hug go a long way. They went fishing with my brother and explored the German forts, not forgetting the cave that we lived in during the crucial hours of war. One thing that really amazed Hans was the abundance of wild berries that blanketed the ground. He picked and picked. Hans and the children also met all my friends as we were invited from house to house. Only the very best was served. The time we spent was far too short, and all too soon we had to say good-bye and drive south again.

We took the return trip through Norway and enjoyed some of the finest scenery the world offers, such as the many waterfalls, mountains, fjords, and lakes. The ferries gave us a nice break in driving. We must have been on about 20 different boats. Whenever we did not stop to visit a friend or relative overnight, we rented a cabin. We could get one for $10–$12 a night. Our cabins had four bunk beds with mattresses. They were very clean and cozy, and had a hot plate so one could make a warm meal. I made a big supper in the evening, a warm hearty breakfast in the morning, and while Hans and the children packed the car, I prepared sandwiches for the noon meal. As we drove, we always found a table for our picnic. In this way we could travel very reasonably. Often we bought fruits and vegetables from the local farmers.

My advice to you is: "Stay away from the beaten path where prices are sky high! But rather go where you will meet the unspoiled natives with down-to-earth prices. In this way you also get the feeling of being in another country."

With a car one can stop and take a look when one sees something beautiful. We stopped often. We saw so many museums, castles, old Viking ships and even Kon-Tiki's raft. There is so much to learn, so much to see. This old world is still filled with wonders. What an education for all of us.

Good-Bye Germany — Hi America

Mutti in Germany was happy to see us again. We spent the last few days there before our return to America. I really was fascinated by the beautiful houses in Germany with all the lovely flower boxes. Everything looked so orderly and neat. The food was excellent. Mutti made something new every day. We never ate the same dish twice.

The two months in Europe flew by, and we returned to our homeland America: Our land, not by birth but by choice. I love the American people, the great country from sea to shining sea. God sent us to this great land. Perhaps there is a reason for it. As we see the lengthening shadows spreading over this nation, the faltering economy, the dim outlook for the future, we hope that we can be of some help. Hans and I learned many hard lessons as we grew up. We know what works and what does not work in an emergency. That was the reason Hans wrote the book, *Timely and Profitable Help For Troubled Americans,* now in its fourth printing. A book written in love, and dedicated to the Americans, the most wonderful people in the world. This book has already been of great help to many. It can be obtained from World Wide Publishing Corporation (P.O. Box 105, Ashland, Oregon 97520-0105) for $9.95 ppd.

Tom and Helen had taken such good care of everything while we were gone, and a few months later they left for Europe. Visiting youth hostels and using a Eurail pass, they traveled through 15 countries. It was a very wonderful experience for them, too.

My Father, The Captain Of The Universe

As I step outside my house at night, I look at the full moon that turns the river into a silvery ribbon. The velvety dark blue sky is just studded with stars. Some of them seem so close that they tempt me to climb a tree to touch them. As I stand there spellbound by all the beauty, a story comes to my mind which I heard many years ago.

The incident happened in the deep South when the paddle-wheelers ran on the rivers. One summer day a fisherman noticed that a small boy came running down to the river, and out on a small landing dock. The lad took his handkerchief and started waving to the paddle-wheeler. "You are crazy," the fisherman said to the little fellow. "That big boat is not going to stop for you." The boy never answered, just kept on waving. To the man's big surprise, the boat came closer and closer. Two strong arms lifted the little boy aboard.

On board the boy looked down on the fisherman and said: "I am no fool, sir. You see, the captain of this boat is my father."

Yes, as I look upon God's handiwork, I realize that the captain of this universe is my Father. A still small voice seems to say: "I am the God of Abraham, Isaac, and Jacob, and I am your God, Inger."

Dear friend, He is no respecter of persons. He can be your God, too, if you ask Him. *"For God so loved the world, that he gave his only begotten Son, that whosoever believeth in him should not perish, but have everlasting life"* (John 3:16). I hope you have enjoyed traveling with me *From The Polar Night To Eternal Light.*

The End.

ORDER FORM
(ISBN Prefix 0-930294)

Below is a partial list of our titles. You may order by filling out this form and sending it to us with payment. Or you may obtain our latest and complete catalog free of charge by sending your request with a SASE to: WORLD WIDE PUBLISHING CORPORATION, Dept PN, P.O. Box 105, Ashland, OR 97520-0105.

FROM THE POLAR NIGHT TO ETERNAL LIGHT

Inger Marie Schneider's life story is a testimony to God's enduring care and love for those who abide in Him. Born and reared in a land where survival in the best of times is hard, her childhood was lived under the harsh deprivations of Nazi occupation. As a young woman she immigrated to the United States and met the challenge of adjusting to a new culture. As wife and mother of a Christian home, Inger's faith has been tested by tragedy, but she has remained steadfast in her love and witness of God. This simple, heartwarming story is a devotional reaching out to troubled hearts. **112 pages. Softcover. $7.95**

SECRETS OF A PROFESSIONAL HOME BUYER by William W. Bell

Practically every American who has any assets or estate at all, or desires to accumulate such, is in need of this book. It will show you how to save a bundle, and start your own wealth-building estate on a shoestring. Buy several of these *perfect "how-to" manuals of low budget home buying during hard times.* They make perfect and permanent gifts for your friends and children. **160 pages. Softcover. $12.95**

TIMELY & PROFITABLE HELP FOR TROUBLED AMERICANS

If you anticipate monetary collapse, a dictatorship and gun confiscation, you must read this book. In it Survival Expert Hans J. Schneider reveals his proven plan for your freedom and SURVIVAL during economic and civil turmoil! 288 pages cover: Self-Sufficiency • Locating Your Place of Refuge • Independent Energy Sources • Inflation-Proof Investments • Alternate Weaponry/Defense Tactics • Wilderness Survival Techniques • Food Tests • Yachting for Survival • Barter Items • Food Preservation/-Storage and much more. Written by one who learned the art of survival from first-hand experience and travels in nearly 100 countries, this manual could mean the difference between life and death during the coming social chaos. **288 pages. Softcover. $8.95**

FLYING TO BE FREE by Hans J. Schneider

"Destined to become a classic in the annals of flying literature!" The day: April 3, 1958. The place: Brussels, Belgium. "One, two, three—contact!" . . . the beginning of one of the most exciting aviation stories ever written.

Hans J. Schneider, among the first German pilots licensed after WWII, flew 4000 treacherous miles in a dangerous aviation mission around Europe and into Africa. With an overloaded 65-h.p. Aeronca Chief and inaccurate maps, he narrowly escaped death a dozen times. Here is Mr. Schneider's *personal*, never-before-told story of years of barnstorming in war-torn Europe, his passionate love for flying, and the dramatic events which changed the rest of his life! This book is a must for everyone who loves to read real-life adventure.

256 pages. Full-color cover. Over 100 photos/illus. $7.95

MASTERS OF LEGALIZED CONFUSION & THEIR PUPPETS

An undisputed eye-opener written without compromise about the spiritual confusion so prevalent today! Read this astonishing, frank work by one who grew up under godless communist occupation when religious worship was taboo, who struggled with a near-fatal sickness, and for many years intensively studied philosophy and religions of mankind (especially Buddhism and Yoga) until he found the simplicity of the Gospel. Written from an uncompromising Biblical standpoint, this exposé has led many from man-made religions into the truth. This book has been translated, read and studied throughout America and the world. Many letters of appreciation have been received recommending it. Written by Hans J. Schneider. **Over 65,000 copies in print! $1.45**

WORLD WIDE PUBLISHING CORP., Dept. PN, P.O. Box 105, Ashland, Oregon 97520-0105 U.S.A. Enclosed is my check/money order. Please rush me:

Quan	Title	Price	Total

Less Discount (3-4 books—10% off, 5-9—15% off, over 10—20% off) _____
BOOKS MAILED PROMPTLY.   Postage/Handling ___1.75___
                                             TOTAL (U.S. funds) _____

PRINT NAME _____

ADDRESS _____

CITY _____ STATE _____ ZIP _____

ALL PRICES ARE SUBJECT TO CHANGE WITHOUT NOTICE.   ALL SALES FINAL.